REINVENTING RUSSIA

The Formation of a Post-Soviet Identity

Peter J. Piveronus, Jr.

University Press of America,® Inc.
Lanham · Boulder · New York · Toronto · Plymouth, UK

Copyright © 2009 by
University Press of America,® Inc.
4501 Forbes Boulevard
Suite 200
Lanham, Maryland 20706
UPA Acquisitions Department (301) 459-3366

Estover Road
Plymouth PL6 7PY
United Kingdom

All rights reserved
Printed in the United States of America
British Library Cataloging in Publication Information Available

Library of Congress Control Number: 2009922986
ISBN: 978-0-7618-4580-5 (paperback : alk. paper)
eISBN: 978-0-7618-4581-2

∞™ The paper used in this publication meets the minimum
requirements of American National Standard for Information
Sciences—Permanence of Paper for Printed Library Materials,
ANSI Z39.48-1992

To Elizabeth

Contents

Acknowledgments	
Preface	vii
Introduction: The Grand Trade-Off	xi
Chapter One: Who Lost Russia?	1
Chapter Two: The Centerpiece of Economic Reform: The People's Enterprise (PE)	9
Chapter Three: Kremlin Capitalism: The Strategic Enterprise (SE)	21
Chapter Four: Eurasianism: The Mackinder Thesis Revisited	33
Chapter Five: The New (Moscow) Consensus	45
Chapter Six: New Russia-New Identity	55
Conclusion: It's All About Economics	61
Postscript: A New Cold War? Russia, the West and the "Near Abroad"	73
Bibliography	81
Index	87
About the Author	97

Acknowledgments

This book is intended as a sequel to my earlier work, *The Reinvention of Capitalism: Russia's Alternative to Corporate Concentration and to the Command Economy*, published in 2006. It was made possible through a generous grant from the Lansing Community College Foundation. In this respect, I should like to express my sincere thanks to the following individuals: Dr. Michael Nealon, Chairperson, the Department of Humanities and Performing Arts; Dr. Gary P. Knippenberg, Dean, Liberal Studies Division; Bill Motz, Chair, Employee Development Fund Committee. Special thanks also go to Ms. Susan Fisher, Director of College Advancement; Pam Bundy; Beth Vanderlip; Ashleigh Taylor; and last but certainly not least, to Ms. Samantha Kirk, Acquisitions Editor, the University Press of America, for her remarkable patience and understanding.

Preface

The recent high price of oil and gas on the world market has highlighted Russia's role as a key energy supplier. In addition, Russia's chairmanship of the Group of Eight most industrialized nations in 2006, and its pivotal role in the attempt to peacefully resolve the crisis surrounding Iran's nuclear ambitions, marks its resurgence as a world force.

In sharp contrast to 1998, when she defaulted on $40 billion in domestic debt and struggled to pay wages for millions of workers, Russia now has the world's fifth largest gold and foreign exchange reserves ($400 billion), and an economy which grew 6.4 percent in 2005, and has averaged 7 percent growth since 2000.* Real wages have increased 9.8 percent, and the RTS, Russia's stock market, up 8.8 percent in 2005, was the world's best performer. The number of Russians living below the poverty line has decreased dramatically from 42 million (28.9 percent) in 2000 to 22 million (15.8 percent) in 2006, a 13.1 percent decline. The middle class, meanwhile, has rapidly expanded to where it now constitutes well over 20 million citizens. Dollar income per capita has risen by nearly 29 percent per annum over the past five years, "faster even," comments *Business Week*, "than in China." Although the average income per person is only $300 per month, "a surprising number of Russians," we are told, "live well or better than their Western counterparts." Matt Donnelly, President of Merrill Lynch & Company and Capgemini, "estimates that 8 million Russians earn at least $2,000, and 3.5 million earn double that." Due to a 13 percent flat income tax, subsidized housing and utilities, and a 10 percent savings rate, 70 percent of all income in Russia is disposable, as opposed to 40 percent for a typical Western consumer. Goldman, Sachs and Company predicts that Russia, by 2025, "will be the world's eighth-largest economy with per capita income of $45,000.[1]"

Russia's sudden resurgence, however, poses a dilemma among the West's political leaders who see the country moving in the wrong direction. Comments *Financial Times* reporter Neil Buckley: "As Russia's renaissance has progressed, so it has moved away from the European democratic model that its

---

*In 2005, real GDP increased by 6 percent; in 2006, it was 6.8 percent; and in 2007, 6.2 percent. For the first time, Russia's GDP passed $1 trillion, placing it among the world's top ten. In August 2006, Russia retired all of its Soviet-era debts worth $22 billion to Western countries. Gold and currency reserves, along with the stabilization fund are nearing $450 billion. Outside the oil and gas sector, meanwhile, the economy is rapidly diversifying. In high-technology industries, employment grew from 330,000 to 1 million in 2007, with revenues expected to increase from $10 billion in 2006 to $40 billion by 2011. Inflation decreased to 9 percent in 2006, hitting the single figures mark for the first time since the collapse of the Soviet Union in 1991. See. Neil Buckley, "Putting the State Back in Charge," *Financial Times* (Russia: Special Report), 20 April 2007, p. 1; also in the same issue, Stefan Wagstl, "Diversification is Elusive Key to Success," p. 2.

former eastern European satellites have largely embraced," prompting a reassessment both in Europe and in Washington as to which direction Russia is headed. "People in the Kremlin regard Russia as culturally a European country," says Vyacheslav Nikonov, a Kremlin-connected political consultant, "which at the same time has no chance of becoming part of the European family. Russia is doomed to become an independent center of power—same as China, India, Japan, the EU [European Union], and the U.S."[2]

As Russia enters the first decade of the new millennium, self confident and assertive in her relations with the rest of the world, she is also in search of a new identity to take the place of the ideology of the now defunct Soviet system. What Russia lacks most of all, comments film producer Alexander Rodnyansky, is "an effective ideology for projecting its influence across its border."[3] Indeed, "[t]he search for identity is the most important issue in Russia today."[4]

The following is a study of the formation of a new national identity in post-Soviet Russia. To do so, we must realize that Russia's recent resurgence is due not only to the current high price of oil and gas, but is also the consequence, in large measure, of the economic reforms of the past twenty years. These reforms, as I have stated in an earlier book, constitute an experiment in binary economics which, through the medium of worker ownership—a core component of binary economics—successfully transformed the Russian economy to a market system, reinventing capitalism in the process.[5] In this regard, Russia's "blue chip" companies will be highlighted to demonstrate how they are part of a "national strategic plan" to prosecute Moscow's interests abroad, utilizing geography (natural resources in the form chiefly of oil and gas), and economics (companies—most of which are minority worker-owned and adhere to binary economic principles—as an arm of Russia's foreign policy), what we shall term, "Geoeconomics."

Closely linked with Russia's "national strategic plan" is the geopolitical theory "Eurasianism" which, like Russia's binary economic experiment, also stresses Russia's uniqueness and argues that Russia need not—indeed should not—Westernize in order to modernize.[6] Just as *Glasnost* and *Perestroika* were the twin doctrines of the Gorbachev/Yeltsin era which witnessed the demise of the Soviet Union, binary economics in its Russian context and "Eurasianism" are the two key principles defining Russia's new identity in the twenty-first century. Together they constitute Russia's "Third Wave" and, as such, form the basis of a new "Russian" or "Moscow Consensus" and pose a direct challenge to the neoliberal policies of the "Washington Consensus" represented by the United States.

Peter J. Piveronus, Jr., Ph.D.
Okemos, Michigan
December 2008

Notes

1. Jason Bush, "Shoppers Gone Wild," *Business Week*, 20 February 2006, pp. 46, 47. Also Neil Buckley, "Selfconfident State Reenters World Stage," *Financial Times* (Special Report: Russia), 21 April 2006, pp. 1, 2. In Russia, although wages are generally much lower than in the West, government subsides help to cover the costs of housing, utilities, transportation, and health care. In terms of the savings rate, the average Russian worker is thus able to accumulate enough disposable income each month to spend on non-essential items. Moreover, with a high savings rate relative to the Western economies (especially in the U.S. where the savings rate is abysmally low), a "domino effect" comes into play. More disposable income for the ordinary Russian worker means more demand for goods and services other than daily household necessities. This, in turn, generates increased demand which, in turn, generates more spending, which sparks (along with increased inflation) further economic growth. It is this dynamic, rather than just the high price of oil and gas on the world market of late (which accounts for 20 percent of Russia's GDP), which may explain much, if not most, of Russia's recent economic expansion.

2. Buckley, "Self-Confident State Reenters World Stage," p. 2.

3. Arkady Ostrovsky, "The Celluloid Search for True Identity," *Financial Times* (Special Report: Russia), 21 April 2006, p. 2.

4. Stefan Wagstyl, "The Country May Look Strong But," *Financial Times* (Special Report: Russia), 21 April 2006, p. 2. "Faced with such sudden disorienting change," writes U.S. Congressional Librarian James H. Billington, "Russians had to rethink their politics, economics, history, and place in the world. In their new state of freedom, they have produced one of the most widespread discussions of the nation's identity in modern history." James H. Billington, *Russia in Search of Itself* (Baltimore and London: The Johns Hopkins University Press, 2004), 48.

5. Peter J. Piveronus, Jr., *The Reinvention of Capitalism: The Russian Alternative to Corporate Concentration and to the Command Economy* (Lewiston, NY: The Edwin Mellen Press, 2006).

6. Charles Clover, "Dreams of the Eurasian Heartland: The Reemergence of Geopolitics," *Foreign Affairs*, 78:2 (March/April 1999): 9-13.

Introduction

The Grand Trade-Off

According to the historian Alfred Crosby, during the 15th and 16th centuries, a broad mutual transfer of diseases, plants and animals took place between the Old World and the New as a result of the European voyages and Spanish colonization. Known widely as "The Columbian Exchange," this great biological transfer changed the lives and diets of three continents, America, Europe and Africa. Partly as a result of the introduction of new crops like maize and the potato, the world's population would double over the next 300 years.[1]

Five hundred years or so later, a second great transfer can be said to have occurred, this time in the realm of economics. During the 1930s, the United States was in the dark depths of the Great Depression. With millions of lost jobs, the future of capitalism was at stake. One-third of the population was living below the poverty line in 1936-37; one-fourth of the work force was unemployed. The U.S. economy, it seemed to many, was on the verge of total collapse. Economists, meanwhile, were faced with the challenge of altering some of their most cherished beliefs.

Soviet Russia, by contrast, was in the midst of an economic boom at the time, due largely to the overall success of Stalin's First Five Year Plan (1928-32) in transforming Russia from a relatively poor, backward, rural, agrarian society into an economic giant capable of defeating powerful Nazi Germany during World War II. According to official Soviet statistics, between 1929 and 1937, the GNP of the Soviet Union increased between 9.4 and 16.7 percent annually. Per capita consumption increased between 3.2 and 12.5 percent during that same period, "figures," writes historian Niall Ferguson, "that bear comparison with the growth achieved by China in the early 1990s." During World War II, the Soviet Union also out-produced Nazi Germany in military hardware. "From March 1943 onwards," Ferguson continues, "the Russians had consistently been able to field between twice and three times as many tanks and self-propelled guns as the Germans. This was remarkable," he exclaims, "given the relative backwardness of the Russian economy and the enormous challenge of relocating production eastwards after the German invasion...." All told, Soviet war production, "accounted for one in four Allied combat aircraft, one in three Allied machine guns, two-fifths of Allied armored vehicles, and two-fifths of allied mortars...The T-34 [Stalin] battle tank was one of the great triumphs of [Russian] design."[2]

Many thinkers, including, among others, Russian commentator, Vladimir Posner, believe that President Franklin D. Roosevelt saved capitalism in America, "by injecting a healthy dose of socialistic programs to correct the excesses of 'free market capitalism,'" which helped, in no small measure, to cause the

Great Depression.[3] Posner's views, in this regard, are supported by Soviet historians Nikolai V. Sivyachev and Nikolai N. Yakovlev. Although they both contend that the influence of Soviet socialism on FDR's New Deal "should not be exaggerated," nonetheless, "it must...be admitted that it did exist. The idea of a planned economy was attractive to many members of the [American] intelligentsia. Unemployed workers discovered for themselves the truth about the possibility of permanent and full employment. The accelerated shift to state-monopolistic formulas as a solution to economic problems, and the trend to liberal social reform, were influenced significantly by the principles of socialism, especially with respect to economic planning and government responsibility for the social welfare of its citizens."[4]

In point of fact, many of those who were affiliated with FDR and New Deal agencies, especially with the Agricultural Adjustment Administration (AAA), were either Communists or fellow-travelers. Commenting on atomic scientist J. Robert Oppenheimer's alleged association with known Communists during the 1930s, authors Kai Bird and Martin Sherwin write: "By 1935, it was not at all unusual for Americans who were concerned with economic justice—including many New Deal liberals—to identify with the Communist movement. Many laborers, as well as writers, journalists, and teachers, supported the most radical features of Franklin Roosevelt's New Deal. And even if most intellectuals didn't actually join the Communist Party, their hearts lay with a populist movement that promised a just world steeped in a culture of egalitarianism."[5]

To historian Richard Parker, reflecting on the views of former Harvard economist, the late John Kenneth Gailbraith, FDR's New Deal represented a willingness "to experiment with alternatives to the traditional theory and practice of market economics."[6] After 1933, what lay ahead for the U.S. was public intervention and planning as the Federal government was utilized more and more to "prime" the economy to generate industrial growth.[7]

In the late 1980s, as Mikhail Gorbachev was in the process of unintentionally dismantling the Soviet system under *Perestroika*, America would reciprocate and the flow of ideas and influences would head in the opposite direction, from the United States to Russia and take the form of Louis Kelso's binary economics. Just as FDR's (depending on one's perspective) "socialistic" New Deal would invigorate the U.S. economy during the 1930s, helping to rescue the American capitalist system from collapse, the application of Kelso's binary economics to Russia's economic reforms would save the Russian economy which was mired in similarly extreme straits following the demise of the Soviet Union in 1991. In fact, it could rightly be said, that binary economics, through the medium of worker ownership, was so significant that it would constitute the centerpiece of Russia's economic reform movement which successfully transformed Russia from a command to a market economy and would become a major factor in Russia's current economic growth.[8] The fact that Russia at present is on the verge of becoming, alongside China, an economic superpower on par with the United States, the European Union, and Japan, is the consequence, in no small respect, of Russia's experiment in binary economics, the core component of which is worker ownership.

The period in which these developments took place was an unsettling time for both the United States and Russia. In Russia, the collapse of Communism and subsequent demise of the Soviet Union left economic liberalism (neoliberalism) in a dominant position as the world's leading economic doctrine, forcing Russia's leaders to reassess the kind of government and society developing in Russia after 1991. In the United States, where neoliberalism had become the reigning philosophy under President Reagan and the first George Bush, increased competition from foreign producers created a crisis of confidence in American business, calling into question the efficacy of the neoliberal economic approach. Neoliberalism may very well result in "a higher standard of living, better services, and more choice" but it had its downside as well. Not only does it bring "new insecurities—about unemployment, about the durability of jobs and the stress of the workplace, about the loss of protection from the vicissitudes of life, about the environment, about the unraveling of the social safety net, about health care and what happens in old age," left unchecked, neoliberalism has produced enormous concentration of wealth creating inequality and social stratification.[9]

First to point out the limitations of neoliberalism was John Kenneth Gailbraith who, in the 1960s, opened the debate among economists "on how democratic societies should organize themselves to achieve goals beyond those offered by the private market." During the 1980s, Gailbraith was a frequent and vociferous critic of Reaganomics which, as he observed, revealed "the outlines of a neo-Darwinian ethic in America's domestic and foreign policies, most easily visible, he stated, 'in the feeling that gifts to the undeserving poor, even to insolvent relatives, are somehow bad for their character.' Social Darwinism also has a comfortable association with one branch of fundamentalist theology, which holds that property expresses God's approval of the worthy." By the start of the 1990s, and especially following the demise of the Soviet Union, markets had become, "the omnipresent, the omnipotent, the omniscient metrics by which all was to be measured. Those who could not [or would not] meet the market's exacting standards [and this included Russia], were either reeducated or abandoned by it." In the meantime, in the U.S., the stronghold of neoliberalism, income and wealth distribution were widening, the American middle class was shrinking, while the poverty-stricken underclass was gradually on the increase, making the U.S. as the new millennium approached, the most inegalitarian of all the advanced industrial societies.[10]

Prior to the 1980s, Marxism-Leninism seemed to provide a viable alternative to the neoliberal economic model of modernization and development, especially for the Third World (LDCs) where, until the end of the 1970s, the Soviet version of socialism and the command economy had made significant inroads. The sudden, unanticipated collapse of the Soviet Union in 1991, however, resulted in the consequent decline (if not demise) of Marxism-Leninism and, along with it, of the command system as both a doctrine and model of modernization and industrialization.

In both the United States and Russia, these profound events created a political climate favorable to the emergence of a new paradigm of economic and social change, out of which came the ESOP (Employee Stock Option Plan) in the U.S. and its namesake, direct worker ownership in Russia. It has also provoked, especially in Russia, a vociferous debate among reformers over what form the new, emerging social and economic system should take and how fast it should arrive.[11] At bottom, in both Russia and the United States, the appearance of worker ownership and the intense debate resulting from it, may help to determine the best way for countries with large economies to distribute wealth in order to achieve social and economic justice.

Worker ownership in Russia emerged from the ideas of San Francisco attorney Louis Kelso who, with Columbia University philosopher and historian Mortimer Adler, published *The Capitalist Manifesto* in 1958, in which they advocate an economic system based on the widespread ownership of capital assets.[12] Patricia Hetter Kelso, the widow of Louis Kelso, and current head of the Kelso Institute for the Study of Economic Systems, informed me during a telephone interview in 2001, that Kelso "was taken seriously in Russia from the beginning [of the reform movement]." Long before *Perestroika*, the Soviet government had *The Capitalist Manifesto*, "translated into every language in the Soviet bloc," and made "available to authorized scholars in the Lenin Library." By 1986, Soviet economists, we are told, were "not only familiar with Kelso's ideas, but fascinated by them." Following the collapse of the Soviet Union, Kelso has remained known "and highly respected in Russia," by both leading academics and officials.[13] In their search for an alternative to the moribund command system, Russia's reformers, after much acrimonious debate, settled on Kelso's binary paradigm as a practical approach to economic reform which satisfied their stated desire both for economic efficiency and social justice.

Binary economics, Norman Kurland writes, "offers a new 'post-scarcity' paradigm for analyzing and correcting structural economic defects [in conventional capitalism], that foster such seemingly intractable problems as global poverty, environmental destruction, and the widening gap between the haves and have-nots." To Kelso, "binary" means "consisting of two parts." Binary economics "divides the factors of production into two all-inclusive, physically interdependent and market quantifiable categories—*human* [labor] and the *non-human* [capital]." The central tenet of binary economics is that, "through the property (or ownership) principle, these two 'independent variables' can link marketable outputs from the labor-capital mix directly to incomes distributed according to market-quantified values of all 'labor' and all 'capital' inputs." According to Kelso's "ownership economics," "there are only two modes by which a person can legitimately contribute to production and thereby be entitled to a commensurate distribution, (1) through his own inputs ('labor' of whatever form), or (2) through his own non-human outputs ('capital' in whatever form)."[14] One way of achieving "ownership economics" is through worker ownership.

What made binary economics so attractive to Soviet economic reformers was its stated commitment to broad-based capital ownership which, under Yeltsin's mass privatization program, allowed most privatized industrial assets to remain in the hands of managers and rank-and-file workers. By turning workers of formerly state-owned enterprises into owners of privatized companies in which they work, the class conflict between owners and workers which, as Marx observed is built into the capitalist system, is largely lessened if not completely eliminated. Under worker ownership, managers are still required to make day-to-day decisions, but are made subject to democratic accountability. Because managers and rank-and-file workers share a common interest, conflict between them is thus reduced. Moreover, worker ownership enabled Russia's privatized enterprises to maximize their competitive edge in the new market economy. To keep costs down, workers were encouraged to keep their wages low, receiving most of their income "by dividing up—as owners—the greater profits that would result."

The role of Russia's powerful trade unions would also undergo change under worker ownership of privatized enterprises. Instead of fulfilling state mandated quotas and mediating worker complaints, "the union would work with owners and management while serving as a check on the power of capital concentrated in the hands of management. The union would protect the ownership rights of non-management workers."[15]

America's connection to worker ownership in Russia began prior to the downfall of the Soviet Union in 1991 and is illustrated by the involvement of two noteworthy non-governmental organizations (NGOs), the Ohio Employee Ownership Center (OEOC) at Kent State University, headed by Professor John Logue and Dan Bell, and the Center for Economic and Social Justice, whose current president is attorney Norm G. Kurland. Both organizations, over the years since Gorbachev's rise to power in the Soviet Union in 1985, have undertaken an active role in promoting both the concept of binary economics and Russian worker ownership and their efforts in this regard have produced significant results.

The OEOC's involvement began in February 1990, when then Ohio governor, Richard Celeste, extended an invitation to Professor Logue to accompany him on a trade mission to Moscow to explore opportunities for Ohio businesses. At the time, Soviet reformers had been requesting that an American expert in worker ownership be sent to Russia. While in Moscow, Logue met with Jacob Keremetsky, a leading advocate of worker ownership, along with trade unionists, plant managers, and academic experts. From these meetings, Logue learned about experiments that were being conducted in worker ownership with worker-leased enterprises. In 1991, following a series of reciprocal visits, an exchange agreement was concluded between Kent State University (home base of the OEOC), and the Russian Academy of Sciences.[16]

Logue's 1990 trip to Russia was to prove the beginning of a lengthy, fruitful partnership between the OEOC and Russian worker-owned companies. In the coming months, 20 Russian general directors were invited to the United States to tour worker-owned companies in Ohio; 16 privatized companies were given ownership training; 200 of their workers were introduced to the advantages of employee training; and 60 Russian trainers were instructed in the use of interactive methods.[17]

In April 1991, the OEOC arranged and hosted a two-week stay by the managers of Mosfurnitura, then a worker-leased, Moscow-based furniture maker, to observe and study Ohio worker-owned companies. The company's director, we are told, "was intent on determining whether employee ownership actually worked, and whether he should stake his career on it." Upon his return to Russia, he had become convinced of the many advantages of worker ownership, and Mosfurnitura was subsequently bought-out by its workers in 1992, becoming 100 percent worker-owned.[18]

In July 1991, Logue and Bell traveled to Russia to observe, first-hand, the BUTEK experiment, an early variant of worker ownership. Created by the USSR Council of Ministers in January 1990, BUTEK was founded by Mikhail Bocharov, who had initiated employee-leasing of former state enterprises. At the time, Bocharov was Director of the Butovsky concern which manufactured construction materials. He was also a member both of the Congress of People's Deputies and the Supreme Soviet of the USSR. Two years earlier, in 1988, with the assistance of Dr. Valery M. Rutgaizur, then an economist at the All-Union Institute for Public Opinion Research, Butovsky became the first employee-leased enterprise in the Moscow region, and, under leasing, began to earn a profit for the first time, which permitted increased salaries for workers and enriched social programs.

BUTEK's creation shifted responsibility for meeting production quotas from the central ministries in Moscow by leasing state-owned enterprises to their workers and allowing them, utilizing market forces, to set their own production goals. The subsequent success of worker-leased enterprises encouraged reformers to legally sanction worker buy-outs of former state enterprises. BUTEK, as the prototype for direct worker ownership with managers and rank-and-file workers as the majority owners of privatized enterprises, was the initial application of binary economics to Russian economic reform.

BUTEK firms became known as "People's Enterprises," the forerunners of the worker-owned enterprises that make up the majority of today's reformed Russian economy. By the end of 1990, 425 companies, employing over 70,000 workers had joined BUTEK with annual sales totaling more than 120 million rubles.[19]

The six enterprises Logue and Bell chose to visit in July 1991, led them to conclude that worker ownership of privatized enterprises through the BUTEK experiment constituted an ideal solution to the problem of economic reform in Russia. Privatization through worker ownership—a key component of binary economics—they observed, "can be carried out quickly, provides powerful incentives for workers to increase production and reinvestment, and its labor-based formula for allocation fits both ideological and cultural norms...What we saw was an impressive demonstration of managerial initiative, improvements in production and compensation (in real terms, at least through July 1991), a significant expansion of existing production capacity and the development of new products, businesses and joint ventures. Production is up, wages are higher, and employees are beginning to accumulate substantial capital." Despite the significant technical and cultural problems that remained—the most intractable of which was "the lack of a culture of ownership among Russian workers"—the "collective private property" that BUTEK promoted, Logue and Bell conclude, "ties capital to labor output," thus meeting an essential requirement of binary economics of a dual income both from earned wages and dividends from capital profits. "Although it can be combined with joint ventures and with foreign firms and investors, its underlying premise has been that privatization," through worker ownership, "should spread productive wealth broadly," and lead to widespread capital ownership called for by binary economics.[20]

Between 1992 and 1994, at the height of Boris Yeltsin's mass privatization program, the OEOC continued to remain an active partner with Russian worker-owned companies, hosting study visits to Ohio for Russian general directors. The OEOC's training programs had been tested successfully in two worker-owned firms—Kazan Electromechanical Plant in the Republic of Tartarstan and Krazny Proletary in Moscow. In 1994 and 1995, Dan Bell, the current director of the OEOC, relocated to Moscow in order to build a Russian worker ownership capacity. In 1996, Olga Klepikova, succeeded Bell as the OEOC's Moscow Office Director. By this time, the OEOC's work in Russia furthering worker ownership had become widely known and admired. A clear indication of the continuing interest in worker ownership by leading Russian officials was the visit in 1999 by a delegation from the Russian Duma as part of a two-week visit to the United States to study American business practices. While here, the Duma delegates made a half-day stay at the OEOC which included a visit to the worker-owned Joseph Industries in Streetsboro, Ohio.[21]

Like the OEOC, the Center for Social and Economic Justice (CSEJ) in Washington, D.C., has also provided substantial support and encouragement to worker ownership in Russia. The CESJ's involvement began in December 1996 when, at the invitation of Dr. Mullanue F. Ganeyev, Duma Deputy and Chairman of the Russian Parliament Commission for Analysis of Privatization Results, Norm Kurland, President of the CSEJ, made an extended visit to Russia. In Moscow, Kurland spoke as a member of a panel, chaired by Dr. Ganeyev, concerned with the consequences of mass privatization. Also on the panel was Dan Bell of the OEOC, and Anatoly Drogalev, head of the Industrial Policy Department of the Moscow City Government. Kurland's presentation included "a ten-point plan for building a new, non-inflationary high growth and high participatory market economy to create ownership sharing and jobs for workers displaced by privatization." He also put forward "an eight-point strategy for shifting the old [command] economy to a market system in a way" which "would allow for sustainable and balanced growth to help close the gap between those at the top and those at the bottom of Russia's economic ladder."

During his stay, Kurland also met with Ivan Goncharov, General Director of the 700 employee Tverskoj Meatpacking Plant (one of the Tver region's largest employers), in Tver to discuss "the possibilities of the 23 percent ownership stake in the enterprise still in the hands of the regional authority." Although at the time of his visit, the enterprise was legally still a worker's collective, "with no shares allocated in the names, of individual workers," every worker, he discovered, had "an account valued in rubles representing the value of his equity in the enterprise earned through a weighted formula based on years of service and salary." Kurland also discovered that the plant was governed by a 30-member board of directors, "half elected by middle management and the other half by the rank-and-file workers" who voted "on a one-person, one-vote basis in a general worker's council." Kurland later gave a presentation to the leaders of the Legislative Assembly of the Tver Region, one of whose members "was a professor at a local university who mentioned that he was instructing classes on Louis Kelso's 'Two-Factor Theory.'"

At the Academy of Labor and Social Relations of the Independent Trade Unions where he was the featured speaker, Kurland gave a two-hour presentation before 50 labor leaders. The Academy, we are told, consists of 200 professors, "mostly Ph.D.'s and 4,000 students." Dr. Nicolay N. Grichenko, the Rector of the Academy, who introduced Kurland as the guest speaker, "later signed a letter authorizing [Kurland] to represent the Academy in seeking support for the Kelsonian approach to privatization."

During the remainder of his 1996 Russian trip, Kurland met with several important officials, including world-renowned eye surgeon, Dr. Svyatoslav Fyodorov, Anatoly Drogalev (mentioned above), and Valery Salkin, former Mayor of Moscow for five years. Fyodorov is described as "a successful entrepreneur who has organized his clinics so that workers participate in management and profits (but not ownership of shares)." Fyodorov also "leads a new centrist party in Russia whose platform supports an economic agenda based on worker participation." Currently, Fyodorov is head of the Russian Union of People's Enterprises (RUPE) whose main goal is "the fostering of favorable economic and legal conditions for the development and effective functioning of worker-owned businesses" throughout the Russian Federation.[22]

Drogalev and Salkin helped Kurland "select three companies from the Moscow City Government portfolio as candidates for [worker ownership] along the lines of CESJ's two-pronged privatization strategy." Kurland "suggested that the City of Moscow use funds available for special demonstrations to allow commercial banks to extend low-cost credit to demonstration [worker-owned] companies," making the point, "that such a demonstration would eliminate subsidies and help generate additional taxable revenues for the City of Moscow."

Before departing Russia, Kurland secured verbal commitments from various policy makers, business and labor leaders and scholars, "to hold an international conference in Moscow on the Kelso (Third Way) model of economic democracy." He was also given authorization "to represent key groups (including the Russian Duma Committee on Review of Privatization Results, and the Academy of Labor and Social Relations of the Independent Trade Unions), before the White House, Congress, the World Bank, IMF, and other U.S. organizations, for the purpose of promoting the Kelsonian approach in Russia's privatization and economic development initiatives."

Summing up his experiences, Kurland noted that although there is "a general consensus among the people he spoke with that Russia's privatization program is very unpopular," he "felt [nonetheless], that there was tremendous openness among most Russians he met to CESJ's Third Way."[23]

The downfall of the Soviet Union in 1991 presented Russia with the opportunity few nations ever experience, to experiment at all levels of society. While the reforms undertaken by Boris Yeltsin in the early 1990s produced chaos and were to prove severely distressful to many if not most ordinary Russians, out of the mass confusion surrounding those highly turbulent years, came a new definition of things, particularly where the economy was concerned. Confronted with the near collapse of the once venerated Soviet system with its cradle-to-the-grave security, Russia's reformers, under the influence of Louis Kelso and binary economics, not only transformed the Russian economy, but, in the process of doing so, reinvented the very nature of capitalism itself. If, as Vladimir Posner and others have commented, the "socialistic" New Deal of FDR during the dark years of the Great Depression can be seen as Russia's "legacy" to American capitalism, binary economics can likewise be viewed, as Kurland and Greaney proclaim, as "America's legacy" to Russian economic reform.

Notes

1. Alfred W. Crosby, Jr., *The Columbian Exchange: Biological and Cultural Consequences of 1492* (New York: Cambridge University Press, 1976).

2. See, Isaac Deutscher, new edition, *Stalin: A Biography* (New York: Vintage Books, 1960), 317-322, for an excellent general view of the Soviet scene during Stalin's First Five Year Plan and the achievements of rapid industrialization; Niall Ferguson, *The War of the World: Twentieth-Century Conflict and the Decline of the West* (New York: The Penguin Press, 2006), 203, 521. The difficulties experienced by the Russian economy following the dissolution of the Soviet Union in 1991 should not obscure the fact that, as recently as 1990, the former Soviet Union remained the world's second largest economy after the United States. Indeed, in 1992, devoid of the republics of the defunct USSR, including industrially rich Ukraine, the Russian economy was still seven times larger than the rapidly expanding economy of China. Historian Richard Parker comments that "when you look at primary production...the Soviets [came] out first globally year after year in things like natural gas, iron ore, and steel." In 1985, he observes, "they produced nearly twice as much steel as the U.S. did. Taken together, all the things Marx, Ricardo, or any other classical theorist of capitalism would tell you are important to industrial success are hallmarks of the Soviet achievement." Parker also points out that between 1985 and 1989, during *Perestroika*, the Soviet GNP grew, according to official statistics, by more than 3 percent a year. "Even by the CIA's much more skeptical estimates, the [Soviet] economy [grew] on average, nearly 1.5 percent—not especially bad considering the tumult that Gorbachev's reforms and the resulting unrest [put] the Soviet's through" at the time. Richard Parker, "Inside the 'Collapsing' Soviet Economy," *Atlantic Monthly* (June 1990), pp. 74, 75.

3. Vladimir Posner, *Parting with Illusions: The Extraordinary Life and Controversial Views of the Soviet Union's Leading Commentator* (New York: The Atlantic Monthly Press, 1990), 278, 279.

4. N.V. Sivyachev and N.N. Yakovlev, *Russia and the United States: U.S.-Soviet Relations from the Soviet Point of View*, trans. by Olga Adler Titelbaum (Chicago: The University of Chicago Press, 1979), 56.

5. Kai Bird and Martin J. Sherwin, *American Prometheius: The Triumph and Tragedy of J. Robert Oppenheimer* (New York: Alfred A. Knopf, 2005), 132, 133.

6. Richard Parker, *John Kenneth Gailbraith: His Life, His Politics, His Economics* (New York: Farrar, Straus & Giroux, 2005), 56.

7. Ibid., 63n.

8. Peter J. Piveronus, Jr., "Direct Worker Ownership: The Russian Formula for Economic Reform," *Essays in Economic and Business History*, XVII (1999): 255.

9. Daniel Yergin and Joseph Stanislaw, *The Commanding Heights: The Battle Between Government and the Marketplace that is Remaking the Modern World* (New York: Simon & Schuster, 1998), 368.

10. Parker, *John Kenneth Gailbraith*, 590.

11. Piveronus, *The Reinvention of Capitalism*, Chapter 3.

12. Louis Kelso and Mortimer Adler, *The Capitalist Manifesto* (New York: Random House, 1958).

13. By the late 1980s, Soviet reformers, like Jacob Keremetsky, a senior researcher at the Institute for the study of the United States and Canada of the Russian Academy of Sciences, had come to realize that worker ownership, a key component of binary economics, was one of the more successful aspects of economic restructuring under *Perestroika*. See, Piveronus, *The Reinvention of Capitalism*, Chapter 3.

14. Norm G. Kurland, "Binary Economics in a Nutshell," unpublished paper (August 2005). See also, Robert Ashford and Rodney Shakespeare, *Binary Economics: The New Paradigm* (New York: The University Press of America, 1999).

15. Norm Kurland and Michael Greaney, "The Third Way: America's True Legacy to Russia and the New Republics," *Social Justice Review* (November/December 1992): 174.

16. Piveronus, *The Reinvention of Capitalism*, 24f.

17. Carol Shaley, *Building on a Dozen Years of Helping Others Become Owners* (Public relations brochure published by the Ohio Employee Ownership Center, Kent State University, Kent Ohio).

18. Piveronus, *The Reinvention of Capitalism*, 25.

19. Valery N. Varvarov, "From State Property to Employee Ownership: The BUTEK Experiment," in John Logue, Sergey Plekhanov and John Simmons, eds., *Transforming Russian Enterprises: From State Control to Employee Ownership* (Westport, CT: Greenwood Press, 1995), 71f.

20. John Logue and Dan Bell, "Worker Ownership in Russia: A Possibility After the Command Economy," *Dissent* (Spring 1992): 203.

21. Shaley, *Building on A Dozen Years of Helping Others Become Owners*.

22. See, The Russian Union of People's Enterprises (RUPE) website, http://rsnp.ru/index en.htn.

23. See, "CESJ Mission to Moscow," *The Economic Justice Monitor*, Newsletter of the Center for Economic and Social Justice, 12:1 (Summer 1997): 6-8. It should be clearly stated that both Norm Kurland and Michael Greaney regard worker ownership as only one facet of binary economics. In their book, *Capital Homesteading for Every Citizen*, Kurland and co-authors Dawn K. Brohawn and Michael Greaney go beyond worker

ownership as such as a means of fully achieving social and economic justice. As Kurland wrote in a letter to me in January 2006: Kelso, he stated, did not focus exclusively on worker ownership, but rather on "universal ownership for every human being" including "interest-free money (i.e., pure credit) and universal access to capital credit as the essential key means for have-nots to become haves." In his view, worker ownership alone does not insure the emergence of a true binary economy as defined by Louis Kelso. Be that as it may, it can scarcely be doubted that worker ownership is one of the key elements of a binary paradigm and was, as I have demonstrated in an earlier book, a principal factor in Russia's economic transformation during the 1990s. See, Norman G. Kurland, Dawn K. Brohawn and Michael D. Greaney, *Capital Homesteading for Every Citizen: A Just Free Market Solution for Saving Social Security* (Washington D.C.: Economic Justice Media, 2004).

Chapter One

Who Lost Russia?

On New Year's Eve 1991, the blood-red and gold hammer and sickle banner of the Soviet Union was somberly lowered from the flagstaff atop the Kremlin (the seat of Communist power for over eighty years), and replaced by the pre-revolutionary white, blue and red tricolor of the newly created Russian Federation. For better or worse, the worker's state created by Lenin following the Bolshevik Revolution in 1917 had come to a sudden, abrupt end.

Although the unanticipated downfall of the Soviet Union—with the possible exception of the tragic conflict in Chechnya—did not bring with it, as many had feared at the time, the ethnic or tribal war experienced by other transitional nations (the disintegration of Yugoslavia is a prime example), the collapse of the Soviet system did produce chaos and misery for millions of ordinary Russians suddenly forced to come to grips with the momentous changes occurring around them. "As a result of the Soviet breakup," comments historian Stephen Cohen, professor of Russian studies at New York University, "Russia...virtually collapsed. During the 1990s its essential infrastructures—political, economic and social—disintegrated. Moscow's hold on its vast territories was weakened by separatism, official corruption and Mafia-like crimes. The worse peacetime depression in modern history brought economic losses more than twice those suffered in World War II. GDP plummeted by nearly half and capital investment by 80 percent. Most Russians were thrown into poverty. Death rates soared and the population shrank. And in August 1998, the financial system imploded."[1]

While over 30 percent of the Russian population sank into poverty, top business and administration elites, writes Jeff Gates, citing from a four-year study conducted by the Department of Elite Studies at the Russian Academy of Sciences in 1994, "reaped enormous profits by leveraging their influence as high-level government or Communist party officials." A report he cites from the September 24, 1994 issue of the *Washington Times* revealed, "that these officials...exploited their connections in an array of state enterprises, banks, factories and government departments to amass an average net worth of $19 million each, plus further millions of undeclared and untaxed income."[2] Across Russian society as a whole, "the differences between social groups [widened]; at the start of 1992, the richest 10 percent earned four times as much as the poorest 10 percent; a year later, they earned 16 times as much."[3]

As tragic as they were for Russia and many if not most of its people, the excesses of what critics have labeled "crony capitalism" should not be overblown. Nor should they obscure the more positive side of Russia's economic reforms of the 1990s, a view that, all too often, is either overlooked or ignored altogether

by observers of the Russian scene. As my earlier book has demonstrated, in addition to successfully transforming the Russian economy
from a command to a market system, Yeltsin's mass privatization program, between 1992 and 1994, produced the most extensive concentration of worker ownership—the centerpiece of Russian economic reform—of any nation in the world, surpassing even the United States where worker ownership was first conceived.[4] Indeed, given the extent of worker ownership in Russia at the end of the 1990s, one could rightly call Russia's economic reform movement of the late 1980s and early 1990s, the largest experiment in democratic capitalism ever attempted.[5]

Washington policy makers, meanwhile, saw Russia's difficulty in making the transition from Communism to capitalism, as America's opportunity. With the Cold War a thing of the past and with it the threat posed to American security and national interests by the now defunct Soviet colossus, fear and loathing of Communism gave way, writes Stephen Cohen, to "unbridled triumphalism" and "[t]he decision to treat post-Soviet Russia as a vanquished nation, analogous to postwar Germany and Japan (but without the funding),"…together with "the bipartisan premise that Moscow's 'direction' at home and abroad should be determined by the United States." Ignoring "Russia's historical traditions and contemporary realities," unbridled triumphalism, by treating Russia as a defeated nation on par with Germany and Japan following World War II, led to "the assumption that the United States had the right, wisdom and power to re-make post-Communist Russia into a political and economic replica of America."[6]

In relation to Russia's economic reforms, American triumphalism took the form of what became known as the "Washington Consensus," an economic strategy which, writes Columbia University economist and Nobel Lauriat, Joseph Stiglitz, "prescribes privatization, fiscal discipline, deregulation and free trade" as the way by which transitional economies, including Russia, should follow to achieve success.[7] Born during the Reagan years, the "Washington Consensus," reached full flower during the two presidential administrations of Bill Clinton. One month following his inauguration, Clinton delivered a speech at American University in which he declared, writes author Morris Berman, "that [America's] challenge was to master the global economy." To achieve this, "American enterprise [read U.S. multinational corporations], needed to operate on a global scale if it was to avoid failure [read expand at all costs or die]. The passage of NAFTA in November 1993," he continues, "…demonstrated the Democratic [Party's] commitment to corporate interests and was hailed by Henry Kissinger as crucial to [U.S.] foreign policy. Clinton's message to China's Jiang Zemin, when the president visited that country in 1998, was that there was no real alternative to the American [neoliberal] system. Indeed, by the end of his second term, the *Boston Globe* was referring to the outgoing President as, 'the pied piper of capitalism.'"[8] The "globalization" strategy that Andrew Bacevich, director of the Center for International Relations at Boston University, claims was U.S. policy in the 1890s has remained true a century later. "Then as now," states Morris Berman, "the goal was to create an integrated order that offered no barriers to the flow of goods, capital, and ideas, and that is administered by the United States. The whole world – [including presumably Russia], is to become a free-market economy...in which the deck is loaded in our favor (globalization = [the "Washington Consensus"] = Americanization)."[9]

In the midst of the acrimonious debate which took place among Russia's reformers in the early 1990s over which direction economic reform should take and how fast it would arrive, Western consultants Jeffrey Sachs, then of Harvard University and Andrus Åslund, Director of the Stockholm Institute of Soviet and East European Economics, arrived in Russia in the late summer and fall of 1991 to attend meetings with Yegor Gaidar, who Boris Yeltsin appointed Prime Minister following the aborted putsch of August 1991, Anatoly Chubais, who was to head up the mass privatization program, and other radical reformers at a dacha outside Moscow to plot the future course of economic reform. Comments University of California, Berkley professor Janine R. Wedel: "It was the springtime of East-West courtship. Russia seemed a blank slate ready for reform; dramatic change was in the air; the West fell in love with the new faces cast from its own ideological mold, and this cadre of 'reformers' [in accordance with the "Washington Consensus"], assumed the role that the West had created for them. They promised quick, all-compassing change that would remake Russia in the Western image and eliminate the vestiges of Communism."[10]

Gaidar was to head those reformers favoring a radical approach to economic reform which conforms to, in the words of former *Financial Times* Moscow Bureau Chief, John Lloyd, "an 'American' conception of economic reform and of economic existence: a form which stresses the freedom and responsibility of the individual and leaves the economy, as far as possible, to the operators of the private actors in it—individuals, companies and voluntary associations such as unions—without state interference."[11] In this vein, Gaidar's approach to Russia's economic transition envisioned a rapid (fast-track) approach to a market system. He urged what became known in reform circles as "shock therapy,"— "the immediate and simultaneous implementation of all reforms" in the shortest time possible.[12]

Sachs and Åslund, both onetime advisors of Poland's economic reforms, emerged as staunch advocates of Gaidar's radical, "fast-track" strategy. "The successful transformation of the socialist economies," they both insisted, "must be based on 'truly radical reform.'" This translated as "shock therapy." [13]

The Gaidar shock therapy formula, whose chief feature was price decontrol, while it gained the enthusiastic support of the World Bank and the International Monetary Fund (IMF), proved disastrous in the end for most ordinary Russians. Price liberalization, which was to have taken place along with other proposed reforms, including a balanced budget and reduced government spending on food subsidies and subsidies for industry, resulted in drastically higher prices for food and other daily necessities and plunged a great many Russians who could not afford them into poverty, while increasing industrial closures raised the unemployment rate and led to a dramatic fall in production. Fierce opposition to this crippling policy from all quarters led to Gaidar's forced resignation from office in December 1992. Yeltsin's subsequent reinstatement of Gaidar under pressure from the IMF which threatened to withhold the balance of a $3 billion financial aid package, followed by his forceful dissolution of the contentious Congress of People's Deputies—a holdover from Soviet times—provoked a violent confrontation between pro- and anti-Yeltsin groups on October 3 and 4, 1993. Ultimately, continued opposition to radical reform compelled Yeltsin to pursue a more "gradualist" policy—one which, in the words of Arkady Volsky, leader of the highly influential (and politically powerful), Union of Industrialists and Entrepreneurs, would not attempt "to duplicate procedures used in other countries," but which, over time, would develop gradually a unique character of its own with little, if any, reference to Western (i.e., American) models. This meant, Volsky insisted, that it was "urgently necessary to strengthen [not weaken, as Gaidar and the radical reformers proposed], state influence on the economy...."[14] In order to secure and maintain the support of the influential enterprise managers and rank-and-file workers Volsky claimed to represent, Yeltsin was forced to revise his reform program so that it would follow a gradualist, social democratic path which was more in keeping with Russian tradition. As subsequent events would soon reveal, the gradualist model, reflected in worker ownership (a key component of binary economics), was the typical ownership form the vast majority of formerly state-owned enterprises assumed once the mass privatization program made its appearance in June and August 1992.[15]

The U.S. Government's strategy for dealing with Russian economic reform after 1992 was the responsibility of Strobe Talbott, Clinton's Assistant Secretary of State and noted Soviet Union expert. Part of that strategy, Talbott reveals, "was to integrate Russia into the community of Baltic and Nordic nations which included NATO allies like Norway, nonaligned states like Sweden and Finland, and [then] applicants for NATO membership like Poland."[16] As point-man for Clinton's Russia policy, Talbott was assigned the task of overseeing the financial aid programs which were intended to support and (not coincidentally), provide direction for Yeltsin's mass privatization program. One such program, already underway at the time of Clinton's inauguration, was to be tainted with scandal.

In 1992, the U.S. Agency for international Development (AID), in the vain attempt to remake Russia in American capitalism's image, awarded a $2.1 million grant to Harvard University. Heading the project was the distinguished economics professor Andrei Schliefer, assisted by John Hay, a Russian-speaking Rhodes Scholar who was to serve as translator. Over the next five years, between 1992 and 1997, Harvard's contracts with AID increased to a total of $57 million as it assumed the task of implementing Russian legal reform and building capital markets.

In May 1997, however, AID suddenly suspended the project accusing both Schliefer and Hay of "[abusing] the trust of the U.S. government by using personal relationships for private gain." Specifically, Schliefer and Hay, together with their wives, were charged with using their connections with Russian authorities to create what was described as "Russia's first mutual fund and a share registry that executes and records mutual fund transactions." Harvard subsequently fired Schliefer, removing him from the project. Three years later, in September 2000, the U.S. Government brought a civil suit against Schliefer, Hay and their wives contending that they defrauded the U.S. government of more than $30 million in AID money that was "paid to Harvard to provide impartial and unbiased advice" in Russia, but instead was used to undercut the purpose of U.S. reform efforts to promote "transparency [and] rule of law," thus teaching the Russians "the opposite lesson: that good connections were more important than fair play." In June 2004, a federal judge found Schliefer and Hay guilty of conspiring to defraud the government by investing in the same financial markets they were responsible for creating. Harvard University was also found in breach of its contract. Based on the suit, Harvard stands to owe the U.S. government as much as $34 million. Schliefer and Hay themselves could owe three times that figure.[17]

Janine Wedel informs us that U.S. officials, in spite of suspicions of corruption, enthusiastically supported what she refers to as the "Chubais Clan [which included Schliefer] as the group that could deliver reform to Russia." The aim, as Schliefer and his colleague Maxim Boyco acknowledged in a 1995 book funded by Harvard, was to "alter the balance of power between [radical free market] reformers and their opponents [the gradualists]" in favor of the radicals. Wedel claims that the economic aid provided by the West (the U.S. in particular), was, in reality, designed not only to further Russia's economic transition, but to give the radical reformers a political advantage over their opponents who were in favor of a slower, more gradual pace to economic reform. "That the chosen Chubais 'reformers' were visibly involved in politics and creating opportunities for themselves," Wedel writes, "opened Western aid to suspicion and skepticism about capitalism, reform, privatization, and the West. Anger has accumulated over the economic 'reforms'—many of them urged, designed, and funded by the United States—reforms that have left many Russians worse off than before the breakup of the Soviet Union." Some Russians, she further states, "now believe that the United States deliberately set out to destroy their economy."[18]

As the chief architect of the "Washington Consensus" during the Clinton years, Talbott, together with Larry Summers—who, in 1991, was appointed chief economist at the World Bank, and who would later take up the post of undersecretary, then deputy secretary, and finally, Secretary of the Treasury— were summoned to testify before a House Congressional panel in the fall of 1998, while Russia was in the midst of a financial crisis, in order to provide answers to the raging debate then in progress over "who lost Russia?"[19]

The scandal surrounding the Harvard University-AID program illustrates that the ongoing and sometimes bitter opposition to privatization in Russia was not due simply to the unsavory activities of the super-rich oligarchs and corrupt political officials, but was inherent both in the perception as well as the motives of the radical reformers and their political cronies. Following the downfall of Communism, the U.S. perceived post-Soviet Russia in the exact same manner as it did the countries of Central Europe. In return for generous financial assistance (which, in Russia's case never materialized to any significant degree), Russia, like the former Warsaw Pact nations, was expected to demonstrate gratitude by a willingness to meet U.S. policy expectations, regardless of the consequences. These expectations, described as a "partnership for peace," were based on the assumption that Russia's reformers would eagerly imitate American economic and political models. American versions of democracy and capitalism were to proceed hand-in-hand with financial assistance. In their seemingly well-meaning but misguided attempt to turn emerging Russian capitalism into a carbon-copy of the neoliberal paradigm favored by the U.S., economic reform in Russia has, all to often, been viewed as the incarnation of "kleptokapitalizm" despite its many accomplishments. If anything, what failed about Russian economic reform was not its goal of transforming Russia into a genuine capitalist system; what brought American advisors like Jeffrey Sachs, who headed the ill-fated Harvard AID project to grief was the unsuccessful attempt to control the course and eventual destination of Russian economic reform in a manner compatible with American political and economic interests in that part of the world. As I have stated in an earlier book, "[I]n their eagerness to transform the Russian economy in America's image with little, if any, concern for the fate of the Russian people, what was ignored or simply overlooked was the need to 'let Russia be Russia'—to allow Russia's reformers to find their own path to a market economy, free from unwanted as well as unwarranted outside influence."[20] Disillusioned and annoyed by their failure, these same advisors, once filled with exuberance over the possibilities (from their standpoint) of Russian economic reform, turned their disappointment and frustration against the reform movement itself, denouncing it as a corruption of what they regard as true, genuine capitalism and labeling it in uncomplimentary terms which resonated with those Russophobes in the Western media (especially in the U.S.) who were eager to use the "Who Lost Russia?" argument as a convenient excuse to revitalize Cold War antagonisms. The end result is an impression of Russian reform—both political and economic—which is hardly favorable and only inhibits our understanding of the reform movement itself by obscuring its actual accomplishments.

Notes

1. Stephen Cohen, "The New American Cold War," *The Nation*, 10 July 2006, p. 9.
2. Jeff Gates, *The Ownership Solution: Toward A Shared Capitalism for the Twenty-First Century* (Reading, MA: Addison-Wesley, 1998), 247.
3. Stephen White, *After Gorbachev* (Cambridge: Cambridge University Press, 1993), 271.
4. Piveronus, *The Reinvention of Capitalism*, 4; also, John Logue and Jacqueline Yates, *The Real World of Employee Ownership* (Ithaca, NY: Cornell University Press, 2001), 1-21; for a critique of privatization see, Grigory Yavlinsky, "Russia's Phony Capitalism," *Foreign Affairs*, 77:3 (May/June 1998).

5. Russia was not the sole transitional economy to experiment with worker ownership. Included among other countries following a similar path were Jamaica, Chile, Poland, Lithuania, and China, to mention a few. However, only in Russia was worker ownership carried out on such a vast scale or had as much impact on the economy and on society. See, "Privatization Through Employee Ownership," *The Journal of Employee Ownership and Finance*, 7:4 (Fall 1995).

6. Stephen Cohen, "The New American Cold War," p. 16.

7. Joseph Stiglitz, "Free Trade Can Be Too Free," *Business Week*, 3 July 2006, p. 102.

8. Morris Berman, *Dark Ages America: The Final Phase of Empire* (New York & London: W.W. Norton & Co., 2005), 142.

Ibid, 143; also Andrew Bacevich, *American Empire: The Reality and Consequences of U.S. Diplomacy* (Cambridge, MA: Harvard University Press, 2002).

9. Janine R. Wedel, *Collision and Collusion: The Strange Case of Western Aid to Eastern Europe* (New York: Palgrave, 2001), 126.

10. John Lloyd, "The Russian Model," *Delovie Lyudi*. 31 (March 1993): 50.

11. Carol Barner-Barry and Cynthia A. Hody, *The Politics of Change: The Transformation of the Former Soviet Union* (New York: St. Martin's Press, 1995), 188.

12. Lynn D. Nelson and Irina Y. Kuzes, *Property to the People: The Struggle for Radical Economic Reform in Russia* (Armonk, NY: M.E. Sharpe, 1994), 38.

13. Ibid, 82.

14. Piveronus, *The Reinvention of Capitalism*, Chapters 4 & 5.

15. Strobe Talbott, *The Russia Hand: A Memoir of Presidential Diplomacy* (New York: Random House; 2002), 67-71.

16. Carla Anne Robbins, "For Harvard Board, Professors Woes Pose Big Dilemma," *The Wall Street Journal*, 12 October 2004, pp. Al, A10.

17. Janine R. Wedel, "Rigging the U.S.-Russian Relationship: Harvard, Chubais and the Transidentity Game," *Demokratizatsiya*, 7:4 (Fall 1999): 492; also, Maxim Boyco and Andrei Schliefer, *Privatizing Russia* (Cambridge, MA: MIT press, 1995); Wedel, *Collision and Collusion*, 125-174. Contrary to what is generally assumed, Russia, between 1991 and 1993, received relatively little financial assistance compared to other emerging countries. Not until 1993 did Russia benefit from the first tranche of a $1.5 billion in untied money from the West "which included $600 million from the World Bank." See, Richard Layard and John Parker, *The Coming Russian Boom: A Guide to Markets and Politics* (New York: The Free Press, 1996), 90.

18. Talbott, *The Russia Hand*, 67-71.

19. Piveronus, *The Reinvention of Capitalism*, 117.

Chapter Two

The Centerpiece of Economic Reform
The People's Enterprise (PE)

Two months prior to the August 1998 financial meltdown which threw the Russian economy into another downward spiral, the Russian State Duma passed Law No. 115, "On the Specifics of the Legal Position of the Workers' Joint-Stock Companies (The People's Enterprises)." In October, what became known as "The People's Enterprise Law" went into effect.[1] Worker-owned companies, which, by the end of the 1990s, would constitute nearly two-thirds of the reformed Russian economy, had won official recognition in the eyes of the law. As a consequence, worker ownership (a key principle of binary economics), symbolized by the People's Enterprise (PE), now constitutes a permanent feature of the Russian economy.[2] Moreover, Federal Law No. 115 not only accords legal status to People's Enterprises, but is intended to prevent, as far as possible, any decline in Russian worker ownership. It is also a clear indication that the Russian Federation government is committed to maintaining and encouraging worker ownership.[3]

A People's Enterprise (PE) is defined as a closely held company which comprises between 51 and 5,000 workers. As such, a PE cannot be either a partnership or a public company. To create a PE requires the votes of three-quarters (75%) of the worker collective.

PE workers are required to own at least 75 percent of the enterprise's stock. Workers who are not stockholders cannot exceed ten percent of the PE's total workforce. An individual worker cannot own more than 5 percent of the PE's total stock, and must sell any surplus shares to the PE for their nominal value within a span of three months. No more than 20 percent of the PE worker's stock can be sold to outsiders. Workers who are dismissed or otherwise terminated by the PE must sell their stock back to the PE at their redemption price and the sale must occur within three months from the time of the worker's dismissal. Stockholders who are not PE workers are required to sell their stocks either to PE stockholders, to the PE itself, or to its workers who are not yet stockholders. The redemption value of PE stocks cannot amount to less than 30 percent of the value of the PE's net assets and, as a rule, must correspond to their market value. The sale of PE stocks cannot exceed 50 percent of the total number of PE stocks earmarked to be sold to the PE's stockholders according to Federal law.

In regard to the governance of the PE itself, stockholders have the right, at a general meeting of all PE workers called for the purpose, to elect on a one-person-one vote basis, the director general (manager) of the PE, together with the chairperson of the supervisory council. They also have the right to determine the numerical size of the supervisory council, its length of service, and salaries. The supervisory council, which exercises authority over the PE, is elected for a three-year term. The general director of the PE and his assistants cannot comprise more than 30 percent of the total numerical composition of the supervisory council. To prevent senior managers from forcing rank-and-file workers to sell them their shares at a low price, strict limits are placed on the transfer of stock from workers to senior managers. The salary of the PE's director cannot exceed 10 times the average worker's pay.

The People's Enterprise was the outgrowth of Boris Yeltsin's mass privatization program of 1992-1994. With Yeltsin in complete control of the Russian government following the defeat of the anti-Yeltsin forces in 1993 (mentioned briefly in the previous chapter), a major obstacle to his reform program had been removed. And yet, in spite of the decisive victory over his opponents in the now disbanded Congress of People's Deputies, Yeltsin had to proceed with caution in implementing his program. His new Prime Minister, Viktor Chernomyrdin, who had replaced Yegor Gaidar, positioned himself as a centrist who, writes Stephen Erlanger, "[was] mostly on the side of the [gradualist] reformers." He "[was] also...more supportive of the state regulation and ownership of key industries," and, like the parliamentary opposition to Yeltsin, argued "that inefficient, post-Soviet industries need special protection against inflation to prevent huge layoffs and subsequent social unrest." [4] He also advocated, comments Russian reporter, Galina Batsanova, "turning existing former Soviet industrial giants into holding companies dealing with everything from raw materials to the sale of the finished product." The Soviet oil and gas conglomerate, Gazprom, which Chernomyrdin created and headed as Minister of Energy under Gorbachev in the late 1980s, was already "one of the most powerful international corporations in the world, with its own banks, exchanges, joint-ventures, and off-shore oil companies with assets not only in Russia and the CIS, but also in Western Europe." When set against the backdrop of the then ailing Russian economy, Gazprom in the early 1990s was "the only bright spark of stability...responsible for one-third of the total hard currency reserves entering Russia." [5]

Yeltsin's stated desire to run for reelection as Russia's president in 1996 made it highly unlikely that he would want to cause additional hardships that would further antagonize the voters. Even some of his erstwhile supporters in the United States at the time, most prominently Senator Robert Dole, then Senate Majority leader, "wondered aloud whether the pace of economic reform [especially under Gaidar], has been too fast for a society that spent seventy-five years under Communism to bear." [6] Pro-Yeltsin officials in the Clinton administration at the time, although they continued to voice their concern over Russia's ballooning inflation rate, and were exasperated because, as they saw things, Moscow was not doing enough to reduce its burgeoning budget, nevertheless, were forced to admit that Russia's economy, despite Gaidar's absence from the Yeltsin cabinet, was "not in desperate shape and had made considerable progress over the last year [1992]." [7]

Notwithstanding the outcome of the violent events of October 3 and 4, 1993 (which were broadcast worldwide), a rapid transition to a Western-style, neoliberal capitalist system, advocated by Gaidar and supported by Harvard University economist and then Yeltsin advisor, Jeffrey Sachs, by the end of 1993, had gone out of vogue among most of Russia's reformers, replaced by the gradualist approach, advocated by, among others, Arkady Volsky, and, ironically, by Boris Yeltsin's now vanquished rivals from the October uprising, Aleksandr Rutskoi and Ruslan Khasbulatov. As Russia's reforms moved forward, out of the chaos of 1992-1993, what had emerged so far from the dismantled command structure of the former Soviet Union, was something akin to a "mixed economy" containing "a substantial state and private sector, but with the state still dominant in large-scale industry, agriculture, transportation, and finance, while private enterprise [flourished] mainly in the services trade and small-scale production." [8]

Worker ownership in Russia (out of which came the People's Enterprise), after 1991 took place against the backdrop of the Russian Federation's privatization legislation of June 1992. This legislation granted employees preference in purchasing voting shares in the state-owned enterprises which were slated for privatization. Also enacted was legislation which called for giving every Russian citizen (man, woman, and child), a voucher that could be exchanged for shares in privatized companies or for cash. [9] Under the June 1992 plan, small enterprises of less than 200 workers and with a value of less than one million rubles (based on the ruble value of January 1, 1992), were to be sold in their entirety, without the formation of joint-stock companies. These were to be sold at auction or through competitive bidding. Enterprises larger than 1,000 workers or valued at more than 50 million rubles were to be privatized by transforming them into joint-stock companies. In all, the 1992 privatization scheme included roughly 20,000 medium-and-large-scale enterprises, all of which accounted for the lion's share of Russia's total industrial capacity. It was, as one writer had said, "the largest single transfer of wealth in modern times." [10]

Two principal privatization options for the conversion of state-owned enterprises were proposed by the government, both of which provoked intense debate among Russia's reformers. In particular, major disagreements arose over the manner in which ownership of enterprise shares should be structured. [11] Of the two options, the one most frequently chosen by the work collectives (managers and rank-and-file employees), was option two which provided for internal or insider (as opposed to external or outsider) ownership and in which a controlling share of the stock is held by insiders, that is, the workers and managers of the enterprise itself. Here, the goal was to assure that workers obtain a significant role both in the ownership as well as the governance of the privatized enterprise. Insider control may include control by the enterprise's managers, by its workers, or by some combination of the two. Worker control can be exercised directly or indirectly through the election of representatives to a worker's council. [12] Employees can purchase 51 percent of the enterprise's stock at 1.7 times the book value of the shares, with voting privileges. Half of the value of these shares could be paid for with privatization vouchers. Unlike option one, employees could actually control as well as own their enterprise. However, they would not receive discounted stocks, and they would not be allowed to pay for their shares in installments. Whatever shares remained would be auctioned by the Property Fund. [13]

By the end of 1993, under Yeltsin's mass privatization program, worker-owned enterprises grew rapidly to where, in terms of their total number, they now constitute a major if not predominant segment of the reformed Russian economy. By the end of 1994, when the first and most crucial phase of the mass privatization ended, approximately 14,000 midsize and large-size state-owned enterprises were privatized as worker-owned companies. This all but dwarfed privatization programs in the Central European countries, including Germany, the Czech and Slovak republics, and in Poland. Indeed, "[t]he speed with which the program has been enacted," comment researchers Ira W. Libermann and Suhail Rahuja, "is impressive given Russia's recent political turbulence and its dire macroeconomic performance." [14]

After years of decline, and despite lingering fears about hyperinflation and the demise of economic liberalization (i.e., neoliberalism), that were voiced following each government shakeup, there were sure signs by the end of 1994, that the mass privatization program—the centerpiece of which was worker ownership—was succeeding and that Russia had finally turned the corner on success. Indeed, there exists ample evidence that the performance of worker-owned enterprises in boosting production may have been, to a considerable extent, along with increased foreign investment, responsible for the growth about to take place. [15] Russia's GDP, the standard gauge for measuring an economy's progress, one Western economist discovered, in dollar terms, soared to $61.4 billion for the first quarter of 1994, implying a GDP for 1994 of $246 billion, compared to $174 billion in 1993. [16] Private consumption, as a share of the GDP rose from a paltry 40 percent—two-thirds being considered normal in the West. Real income rose by no less than 9 percent in 1993; registered retail sales expanded by 2 percent, which Swedish economist Anders Åslund felt at the time were most likely underestimated. [17] Increased sales of individual products, especially consumer durables, were most impressive. Sales of television sets, for example, surged 34 percent. "Refuting ideas of approaching famine," Åslund observed, was the 46 percent share of family budgets spent on food. Throughout the Russian Federation as a whole, a construction boom was underway for individual family homes, a good indicator that Russia was in the process of changing from a society predominantly of apartment dwellers into a country of individual home owners, a sure sign of the rise of a prosperous middle class. The home construction boom spread to Siberia where, by 1994, one in three families were building homes. [18] In addition to home construction, the Russian auto industry expanded as the total number of automobiles owned by Russians increased 9 percent in 1993 and increased again in 1994. [19]

Åslund's optimistic conclusions about the success of the mass privatization program in promoting Russia's economic growth were shared by the findings of *The Economist*.[20] Moscow, in 1994, it was discovered, had all the markings of a classic boomtown. After a precipitous drop in productivity between 1990 and 1993, when industrial production was cut in half, by the mid-1990s, there were definite signs that the decline in industrial output had reached bottom. In October 1994, after surviving a vote of no confidence, Prime Minister Chernomyrdin introduced the Russian Federation budget for 1994-1995 to the State Duma citing the accomplishments of the past year and outlining future projections for the Russian economy. According to his findings, industrial production in October 1994 showed a rise of 15 percent from the previous month and a 6 percent increase from a year earlier. By the end of 1995, Chernomyrdin's earlier prediction of limiting inflation to between 1.5 to 2 percent per month had been met.[21]

As a consequence of privatization-cum-worker-ownership, the private sector of the Russian economy, by 1995, produced 58 percent of the country's official GDP which, in June 1994, stood at 364 trillion rubles, or $245 billion at the average exchange rate for the period. Between January and July 1994, real household incomes rose by 18 percent, while real household consumption increased by 10 percent. Savings were also up. In July 1993, Russian households had 1.6 trillion rubles ($1.5 billion) on deposit at banks. One year later, in July 1994, that figure shot up to 14.8 trillion rubles, or $7.4 billion, giving Russians one of the highest personal saving rates in the developed world.

Critics had been complaining about Russia being forced to live on imported food because of critical food shortages at home; and yet, for the first months of 1994, although imports of chicken and red meat displayed a marked increase from 90,000 tons in January to almost 400,000 tons in August, Russia actually enjoyed (and still enjoys today), a trade surplus of $11.7 billion. Inflation, although high by Western standards, leveled off to between 4 to 8 percent per month. By August 1994, the spiraling inflation rate was brought down from 21 percent in January to 4.5 percent. In September, however, it increased to 7.7 percent due to a state-sponsored loosened monetary policy. In the 1994-1995 budget presented to the State Duma, Chernomyrdin predicted a quick inflation surge to about 15 percent in October, but forecasted that the rate should drop to 5 percent per month in November and December.[22]

As for ordinary Russians, *The Economist* discovered that, in 1994, they were living far better than the gloomy official statistics suggested. One reason is that Russians, on average, pay much less for basic necessities than do their counterparts in the West. Even though prices for basic services like rent, heat, water and gas, rose sharply due to increased inflation, they still represented only a fraction of the cost of delivering these services to consumers. For this reason (as was indicated in the preface), the proportion of disposable income in Russia was then, and still is, far greater than in many Western countries. As a result, the number of people living below the poverty level was cut in half, from slightly over 40 million in June 1993, to 20 million by June 1994. According to Russian Labor Ministry statistics, for the first half of 1994, the income differential between the richest 10 percent of the Russian population and the poorest ten percent was 1 to 7.4, down from 1 to 11 in January. [23] "A massive redistribution of income is taking place" in Russia, comments Åslund, and although income differentials "have widened, they are still smaller than in the United States." [24]

One of the most significant results of privatization since 1992 has been its profound impact on Russian society. According to a survey conducted by *Argumenty I Facty*, Russia, by 1994, was turning into a nation of middle class citizens, due primarily, in its opinion, to the economic reforms then in progress. The popular weekly newspaper defined between 25 and 30 percent of all Russians (approximately 50 million citizens), as middle class, earning monthly salaries of up to 500,000 rubles (about $250). An additional 5 percent of the population, about 9 million citizens, fell into the upper middle class, earning more than 500,000 rubles a month, while more than 2.5 million Russians, or 3.5 percent of the population, qualify as "ruble millionaires," with monthly incomes of $1,000 to $1,500. [25]

Another important consequence of privatization has been the emergence and growth of the Russian stock market (RTS), which, by August 1994, had become the chief source of new capital, replacing state investment. By 1995, the Russian stock market had a total capitalization of over 90 million rubles. According to the Ministry of Privatization, since the start of 1994, over $500 million per month had flowed into the Russian market, most of it coming from foreign investors. For American and other foreign investors, writes journalist Richard Stevenson, "Russia [in 1994] present[ed] a business opportunity so big that they [could] no longer afford to hold back." [26] Since Russia completed its first round of privatization on June 30, 1994, "money [poured]...into the country...from foreign companies and investment funds that had previously been scared off by the near chaos of Russia's political and economic transition." American direct investment in Russia, which was practically nil at the beginning of 1994, had been projected to reach $50 billion in the next ten years. Dan Lubash, an analyst who then tracked Russia for Merill Lynch, commented that "the actual wealth behind the Russian economy is tremendous." Danielle Downing, then director of Russian investments at C.A. & Company, a Russian-owned brokerage firm, expected emerging market funds from the United States, which were at the time, experiencing rapid growth, to begin allocating up to 12 percent of their assets in Russia, "making Russia one of the largest targets for investment of that type." [27]

A major source for foreign investment in Russia has been in the area of international joint ventures. In a study Professor Vladimir Kvint of Fordham University conducted of joint ventures attempted in Russia between 1989 and 1994, it was discovered that between 35 and 38 percent of consummated joint ventures "[were] already profitable or well on their way. That [was] the highest success rate for new businesses in the world," contradicting the oft-mentioned complaint that Russians have been unduly hostile towards foreign corporations operating in Russia. According to Professor Kvint's findings, by early 1994, there were more than 18, 000 joint ventures in Russia representing more than $10 billion in foreign investment. The largest foreign joint venture partners, at the time, were from the United States and the European (EU) countries, chiefly Germany. [28] Between January 1992 and January 1994, the number of U.S.-Russian joint ventures increased dramatically from a mere 625 to 2,800. Professor Kvint's study also found that approximately $1 billion in U.S. investments flowed into Russia between October 1992 and December 1993, at a time when economic and political uncertainty was at its highest. Many of the largest American companies, including IBM, General Electric, Ford, Hewlett-Packard, Eastman-Kodak, Platex, Chevron and AT&T, by 1994, were already on location. In addition to the big corporations, thousands of small and medium-size ventures had also arrived. Most of the joint ventures, Professor Kvint informs us, were in software, heavy industrial production, tourism and hotels. "There [was] also...an explosion in the growth of research and development" and companies such as Bell Labs are today cooperating with Russian scientists to study space, electronics, optics, lasers, and nuclear energy. [29]

Russia's economic revival of 1994 to 1997, sadly, was followed in August 1998 by a financial crisis which, once again, plunged the country into chaos. Throughout it all, however, worker ownership continued to hold its own, remaining at the core of Russia's reformed economy. By January 1996, there were 118,797 privatized companies in the Russian Federation. Out of these, the vast majority (about two-thirds), were registered as worker-owned companies. In 1995 and 1996, option two of the 1992 privatization scheme, where employees could buy up to 51 percent of company stock, was chosen by 72.5 percent of the work collectives, a fact that reveals that between 1994, when the first and most crucial phase of Yeltsin's mass privatization program ended, and 1996, the privatization of most state-owned enterprises continued to emphasize worker ownership as the principal ownership form. [30] By 1996, Professor Joseph Blasi of Rutgers University discovered that workers of all kinds in Russia, still possessed majority ownership in almost two-thirds (64.7%) of those state enterprises which were privatized. He was also surprised to find that worker ownership, in 1996, was actually on the rise—"at least there was no evidence of an across-the-board decline in average employee ownership, or in the number of firms whose employees had majority control." Although outside ownership showed a slight increase in 1995 and 1996—32 percent average nationwide; 19.8 percent majority ownership—"a quarter of all privatized companies have much less than the national average of outside ownership." [31]

In March 2002, John Simmons, then president of Participation Associates in Chicago, in an address to the Kennan Institute at the Woodrow Wilson Center in Washington D.C., reported that in a number of worker-owned enterprises across Russia a full-fledged revolt was in progress over a government decree which allowed outside investors to control up to two-thirds of a company's board of directors even though workers control the vast majority of the shares. [32] Outraged workers in several of these enterprises, in response, resorted to direct action and, in some cases, have forcibly taken back their plants, locking-out corrupt directors and replacing them with directors elected by the workers. [33] These so called "protest firms" attracted the attention of the State Duma in Moscow which, in recognition of the worker's grave concerns, established in 2000 at the height of the worker protests, The Center to Study Protest Firms.

Simmons also discovered, much to his dismay, that a great many privatized enterprises were plagued by corruption and mismanagement, what is termed, "predatory privatization" which gravely threatens the future of the Russian economy. Be that as it may, data suggests, he points out, that a powerful anti-corruption strategy exists in "broad-based employee participation in ownership and decision-making that also leads to improved performance." He cites several examples of how worker-owned companies have radically changed the way in which they are managed and, by so doing, have become more productive and cost-efficient. Elinar, a worker-owned company located in Atepsevo, a village 100 km. south of Moscow, is among the more successful of these enterprises. "So many people from around [Russia] came to see Elinar's success that they had to stop taking visitors two years ago [2000]. Ninety percent of the share-holders are employees in the factory and farm who vote to select the boards which choose the General Director." Druzba, a nearly bankrupt collective farm, was purchased by Elinar in exchange for the farm's 800 workers and 3,000 acres. In two years from the date of its purchase, we are told, Druzba became the top Russian producer in the Moscow poultry market, achieving this result "using self-managing work teams and paying bonuses based on gain-sharing methods." Indeed, so successful was Elinar that "foreign investors added $20 million to expand their production." [34]

Energia in Voronezh and Konfil, a chocolate candy company in Volgograd, are other examples Simmons uses in his report of highly successful Russian worker-owned enterprises. Konfil's 500 workers, in 1998, voted to become one of Russia's earliest People's Enterprises, hoping that this would avert a planned hostile take-over by criminal elements. "Since then," Simmons writes, "sales have increased, along with employee participation in decision making." In 1997, a second shift began operating, and when Simmons visited the plant in December 2000, "a third shift had gone into operation."

Four years after the passage of the People's Enterprise Law by the State Duma, a follow-up law was enacted "that encourage[s] the sale of the shares that the government holds to the employees in firms where [they] hold 51 percent of the shares. Today," Simmons continues, "about 25 percent of the joint-stock companies formed under the privatization law [of June 1992] have majority employee ownership. The new law," Simmons predicts, "could quickly expand the number of closed firms with broad-based employee ownership." [35]

In concluding his study of enterprise transformation in Russia, Simmons observes that in order to become and remain competitive, Russia's privatized enterprises must focus on quality and broad-based ownership and participation management. He cites studies made over the last 50 years by Peter Serge of MIT and by Tom Peters, the McKinsey consultant and author, which demonstrate that "participation in management and ownership has accelerated productivity improvement and contributed to the steady expansion of the GDP of a growing number of countries." These include, it should be emphasized, Russia, whose high economic growth rate of the past several years, especially since the dawn of the new millennium, must be attributed to the success of its worker-owned People's Enterprises.

Clearly, despite ongoing problems of widespread corruption and mismanagement, and the restructuring of privatized companies to include outside owners, worker ownership continues to characterize most of the former state-owned enterprises which were privatized since 1992. All things considered, there is general agreement among most experts in the area of Russian worker ownership, "that employee ownership will continue to play a significant role as a form of ownership [in Russia] for some years to come."[36]

Notes

1. See, Piveronus, *The Reinvention of Capitalism*, Appendix B
2. See, Sergey Mitsek, "The State of Employee Ownership in Russia," *The Journal of Employee Ownership and Finance*, 10:4 (Fall 1998): 135-139. The actual number of majority worker-owned companies in Russia currently is a matter of debate. Mitsek reports a sharp decline in majority worker ownership between 1992 and 1997 from 58 percent to less than 40 percent. Viktor Supyan, on the other hand, has discovered a much smaller decrease—from 67 percent in 1993, to 58 percent in 1996. If managers, along with rank-and-file employees are included as "stakeholders," the decrease in majority worker ownership is smaller still. See, Viktor Supyan, "Privatization in Russia: Preliminary Results and Socioeconomic Implications," *Demokratizatsiya*, 9:1 (Winter 2001): 137-150.
3. For Putin's attitude toward worker ownership, see, Piveronus, *The Reinvention of Capitalism*, Chapter 8, pp. 98f
4. Steven Erlanger, "Now That Parliament's Gone, Can Yeltsin Really Reform Russia's Economy," *New York Times*, 6 October 1993, p. A5.
5. Galina Batsanova, "Stepping Out of the Shadows," *Delovie Lyudi* (January/February 1993): 15. In this sense, Gazprom can be seen as the forerunner of the "Strategic Enterprise" (discussed in the following chapter), which would emerge under Yeltsin's successor as president, Vladimir Putin in an attempt by the Russian Federation government to reverse the excesses of the Oligarchs and regain control over the Russian economy's "commanding heights," especially the lucrative oil and gas sector.
6. Steven Erlanger, "West is Welcoming Reformers' Return in Moscow," *New York Times*, 17 September 1993, p. 4.The title of Erlanger's article is in reference to Yeltsin's reappointment of Gaidar as Prime Minister which, as we noticed, helped spark the October uprising.
7. Steven Greenhouse, "IMF Delays $1.5 Billion Loan to Russia Because Reform is Stalled," New York Times, 20 September 1992, p. A3.
8. Stephen Cohen, "American Policy and Russia's Future," *The Nation*, 12 April 1993, p. 480; also in the same issue, David M. Katz, "The Cure that Could Kill," pp. 514-516.
9. Celestine Bohlen, "Russians to Share State's New Wealth in Start of Shift to Capitalism," *New York Times*, 1 October 1992, pp. 1, A6; also by the same author, "Yeltsin Outlines Plan to Sell Industry to Russians," *New York Times*, 20 August 1992, p. A4. Yeltsin intended to make privatization vouchers the main thrust of his revised economic

reform program. Advocating a kind of "People's Capitalism," he argued that Russia needs "millions of owners rather than a handful of millionaires...The privatization voucher is a ticket for each of us to a free economy." See, "The President's Address to Citizens," *Rossiiskaya gazeta*, 20 August 1992; "B.N. Yeltsin's Speech," *Rossiiskie vesti*, 25 August 1992; also, Piveronus, *The Reinvention of Capitalism*, Chapter 4.

10. Ira Liebermann, Suhail Rahuja, "An Overview of Mass Privatization in Russia," Working paper presented at the World Bank Conference, Washington, D.C., 21 June 1994. Also, "State Program for the Privatization of State and Municipal Enterprises of the Russian Federation for 1992," *Rossiiskaya gazeta*, 9 July 1992; Piveronus, The Reinvention of Capitalism, Chapter 5.

11. Thomas E. Weisskopf, "Myths and Realities of Privatization in Russia," *Review of Radical Political Economics*, 26:3: 32; also, Alexander Binn, Derek Jones and Thomas Weisskopf, "Privatization in the Former Soviet Union and the New Russia," *Privatization in Central and Eastern Europe* (New York: Longman, 1994), 261-267; Piveronus, *The Reinvention of Capitalism*, for a detailed description of the two options (Chapter 5).

12. Weisskopf, "Myths and Realities of Privatization in Russia;" 40n.

13. Nelson and Kuzes, *Property to the People*, 125-127.

14. Ira W. Libermann and Suhail Rahuja, "An Overview of Privatization in Russia," in Ira W. Libermann and John Nellis, eds., *Russia: Creating Private Enterprises and Efficient Markets* (Washington, D.C.: The World Bank: The Private Sector Development Department, 1994), 7, 8.

15. Anders Åslund, "Russia's Success Story," *Foreign Affairs* (September/October 1994): 66; Layard and Parker, *The Coming Russian Boom*, 226-316.

16. Claudia Rosett, "Figures Never Lie but They Seldom Tell the Truth About the Russian Economy," *Wall Street Journal*, 1 July 1994, p. A12; also, Steve Liesman, "Russia's Economic News: It's Not All Bad," *Wall Street Journal*, 28 November 1994, p. A14.

17. Åslund, "Russia's Success Story"; Layard & Parker, *The Coming Russian Boom*, 226-316.

18. Layard and Parker, *The Coming Russian Boom*, 226-316.

19. Ibid.

20. "Russian Capitalism: Under New Management," *The Economist*, 18 October 1994, pp. 21, 22.

21. Adi Ignatius, "Chernomyrdin Survives Votes of No Confidence," *Wall Street Journal*, 28 October 1994, p. A10.

22. Ibid.

23. "Russian Capitalism: Under New Management," pp. 21,22; Douglas Herbert, "Radio Advertizers Tune in to Russia's Middle Class," *New York Times*, 15 August 1994, p. C5. According to Russian Economic Trends, in 1991, the person 10 percent from the top had an income 3 times as high as the person 10 percent from the bottom of the socioeconomic scale. By 1994, the difference had risen 5.5 times, which is approximately the same degree of inequality as in the United Kingdom, although, according to Layard and Parker, the latter figures are probably exaggerated. See, Layard and Parker, *The Coming Russian Boom*, 111, 112.

24. Åslund, "Russia's Success Story:" 66.

25. Herbert, "Radio Advertizers Tune in to Russia's Middle Class," p. C5.

26. Richard W. Stevenson, "Foreign Capitalists Brush Risks to Invest in Russia," *New York Times*, 11 October 1994, pp. C1, C4.

27. Ibid.

28. Vladimir Kvint, "Don't Give Up on Russia," *Harvard Business Review* (March/April 1994): 62, 66; also by the same author, *The Barefoot Shoemaker: Capitalizing on the New Russia* (New York: Arcade Press, 1993). For a more recent view, see, "The Scary Business of Russia," *Forbes*, 23 May 2005, p. 42.

29. Kvint, "Don't Give Up on Russia," 66.

30. Alfred Kokh, *The Selling of the Soviet Empire: Politics and Economics of Russia's Privatization: Revelations of the Principle Insider* (New York: S.P.I. Books, 1998), 145, 146. In 1997, Kokh was appointed by Yeltsin Deputy Prime Minister in addition to his position as Chairperson of the Russian Federation's State Committee of State Property. At the time of publication, Kokh had stepped down from his political positions.

31. Joseph Blasi, Maya Kroumova and Douglas Kruse, *Kremlin Capitalism: Privatizing the Russian Economy* (Ithaca, NY: Cornell University Press, 1997), 55.

32. John Simmons, "Transforming Russian Enterprises: Performance, Ownership, and Performance," Washington D.C.: The Kennan Institute, March 4, 2002.

33. See also, Piveronus, *The Reinvention of Capitalism*, Chapter 8.

34. Elinar and Druzba are also examined in Ibid., Chapter 6.

35. A follow-up survey of privatized enterprises in 1994 by the Russian Privatization Project revealed that majority worker-ownership in Russia which stood at slightly over 90 percent in 1992 when the initial survey was taken, had decreased to 60 percent by 1994. Minority worker ownership, on the other hand, had increased during the same period to 40 percent from 9 percent. Professor Joseph Blasi predicted, based on these results, that majority worker ownership in Russia would most likely continue to decrease after 1994, falling below 30 percent, with many worker-owned companies averaging below 20 percent. Growing minority worker-ownership would place Russia on par with the U.S. economy where, says Blasi, it is "considered a novel and interesting development in a free market economy" which, he predicts could very well "create another large economy with significant minority worker ownership." Blasi, Kroumova & Kruse, *Kremlin Capitalism*, 55.

36. See, Piveronus, *The Reinvention of Capitalism*, Appendix C.

37. Logue, Plekhanov and Simmons eds., *Transforming Russian Enterprises: From State Control to Employee Ownership*, 262.

Chapter Three

Kremlin Capitalism: The Strategic Enterprise (SE)

Until recently an all-too often overlooked fact about Russia's economy is the potential to be derived from its enormous wealth of natural resources. The World Bank estimates that Russia has the world's largest reserves of gas, coal, and aluminum, the second largest deposits of gold, nickel and timber, and the third largest reserves of oil and diamonds. Writes financial analyst John Thornhill of the *Financial Times*: "Russia's 'natural wealth' is 2.5 times as big as that of the next three largest countries combined. Seven decades of perverse economic planning in Soviet times largely suppressed that potential, but it now seems only a question of time before economic gravity exerts its pull."[1] As Russia's economy rebounded from the disastrous effects of the August 1998 crisis, one result was Russia's reemergence as a world economic power.

A good indicator of Russia's return to global economic status has been the appearance of the Russian transnational company and its expansion into the global marketplace alongside Western and Japanese transnationals. "Combined with fearsomely aggressive managers and hungry ambition born of decades of deprivation, Russia's biggest companies," comments Thornhill, "could emerge as giants on the world business stage. If they do, well-positioned investors could be in for the ride of their lives—although they should be aware," he cautions, "of Russia's unique characteristics which are likely to make its future transnationals unlike any other the world has so far seen."[2] Emerging markets guru Mark. J. Mobius likewise cautions: "You may be sitting in an industry that is going to be taken over by a Russian company in the future, or whose market is going to be dominated in the future by a Russian company. We have to start dealing with this new player on the world scene. We're getting a much more effective management. It's a whole new ballgame."[3]

Leading the way by far among Russia's transnationals is the gas giant, Gazprom, "far and away," writes Professor Thane Gustafson of Georgetown University, "Russia's richest and most powerful company."[4] As such, Gazprom is one of four basic industries which together comprise the framework of Russia's economic infrastructure, the other three being railroads, telephones, and oil pipelines. "In Russian parlance, this group is referred to as the 'natural monopolies.'"[5] Described as "the flagship of the [former] Soviet economy," Gazprom is now hailed as "Russia's brightest star."[6] As one of Russia's "blue-chip" companies, Gazprom is also what has been termed a "strategic enterprise" (SE), part of a "national strategic plan," an instrument of Kremlin policy both domestically and abroad.

Gazprom was created out of the Soviet gas ministry in 1989 by Viktor Chernomyrdin, post-Soviet Russia's long-time Prime Minister, as a state-owned enterprise. In June 1992, as part of Yeltsin's mass privatization program, it was made into a joint-stock company. In 1994, 50 percent of Gazprom's stock was divested, "15 percent went to employees and the inhabitants of the main gas-producing region; the population of the Yamal-Nenets region, where the largest fields are or will be, were given a special tranche of over 5 percent. The bulk of the stock was sold to domestic investors, none of which appears to have substantial influence on the company."[7]

Currently the world's largest gas company, Gazprom controls 22 percent of the world's reserves. It has control of almost all of Russia's natural gas and produces 33 percent of the world's natural gas production. Gazprom also enjoys a monopoly on the export of natural gas from Russia. Through its 90,000 mile network of pipelines, which run west from remote fields near the Arctic Ocean in Western Siberia, Gazprom is the main supplier of natural gas to Western Europe, supplying (in 1995) 2 percent of its natural gas consumption and 55 percent in Eastern Europe. In 1994, Gazprom's estimated net income was $1.6 billion on revenues of $10.6 billion, increasing in 1995 to $3.4 billion on revenues of $15.9 billion. Its net income in 2005 was $11 billion on revenues of $48.9 billion. It has issued 23.7 million shares with 51 percent held by the Russian Federation government. In October 1996, Gazprom was the first Russian transnational to be listed on the London Stock Exchange.[8]

With hard currency exports in excess of $8 billion a year, Gazprom is Russia's largest company, accounting on its own, for some 8 percent of Russia's entire GDP. Gazprom's gas reserves, according to MC Securities, a London-based stock broking group, are estimated to be 24 times as large as those of Royal Dutch Shell, and 28 times those of Exxon. Writes John Thornhill: "It comes as little wonder that Gazprom employees [who control 15 percent of the company as was noted], say you can see the whole of Russia from the top of the company's towering new headquarters in Moscow."[9]

Gazprom, we are told, "wields a great deal of political power in Russia." Viktor Chernomyrdin, Yeltsin's one-time Prime Minister, was (as was noted), a former Gazprom chief (Alexei Miller, a Putin favorite, is currently CEO). Putin's intended goal of exerting more state control over the so called "commanding heights" of the Russian economy was anticipated by Chernomydrin's policy of converting then existing Soviet industrial giants—including Gazprom—into holding companies which could deal with everything from raw materials to the sale of the finished product. "While not returning to Soviet-style central planning, Russia," observes reporter Neil Buckley, "is moving towards a model of state-controlled or at least Russian-controlled 'champion companies' [read, strategic enterprises] in sectors that are growing [oil and gas in particular], or where Russia has a competitive advantage with a state-directed policy for each sector." The men around Putin, "would take control of key sectors—oil and gas, metals and minerals, and parts of defense and aerospace—and use these as motors for growth." Foreign companies will be encouraged "to take minority stakes to import technology and expertise... [but] foreign control in strategic sectors or even 50-50 ventures...may be out."[10]

As a Strategic Enterprise (SE), Gazprom had become, under Putin, part of a "national strategic plan" whose use as an instrument of Russia's foreign policy, is to further Russia's economic interests abroad. Since the 1970s, and even more so recently, Gazprom has played an increasingly assertive role in the Western Europe gas market and has succeeded in obtaining sizeable market shares in all of Western Europe's most populous countries. In Germany, Russian gas accounts for 46 percent of the gas market; in Italy, 45 percent; and in France, 37 percent. In addition, Gazprom maintains joint-venture gas transportation and marketing operations in 10 other European countries. In 1994, Gazprom acquired a 25 percent stake in Finland's gas distribution network, after forming a joint-venture with Neste, the Finnish state enterprise. Gazprom also has plans to expand into the British market by purchasing a 10 percent interest in the $700 million interconnector pipeline which British Gas constructed to sell its surplus gas to Europe. Gazprom is hopeful that it can reverse the pipeline's flow when Britain becomes a net importer of gas sometime in the next ten years.[11] With the import market for natural gas expected to rise from 156 billion cubic meters in 1995, to 322 billion cubic meters by 2010, Gazprom, "seems at least well placed as any of its rivals to meet the increased demands for gas....Already Gazprom has advance orders for 160 billion [cubic meters] of gas over the next 15 years."[12] Moreover, Gazprom management's well-thought policies, by concentrating on increasing the liquidity of the company's stock, have made Gazprom shares a very good buy both to foreign as well as to domestic investors.

Gazprom is not only Russia's largest, most important company. Like the smaller worker-owned companies in Russia, "[i]t has also inherited," write reporters Andrew Kramer and Steven Meyers, "its piece of the Soviet Union's paternalistic economy in towns and settlements stretching from the Arctic gas fields to those along the maze of pipelines leading south."[13] Place-centered and committed to the maintenance of social partnerships which obligate it to provide social welfare, Gazprom retains and is in the process of acquiring "shipping lines, an airline, farms, food processing plants, hotels and bottling factories—many of them serving the needs of its 360,000 employees and the 6 million people who are largely dependent on it."[14] The many social partnerships which Gazprom maintains are what it calls "cooperation agreements" with local authorities in distant regions of the Russian Federation. It has played a large role in converting Soviet military factories to civilian use, helping to boost the local economy by purchasing equipment and services from local companies, including underutilized defense plants, in return for their help in collecting receivables from Gazprom's local clients. All told, more than one-fifth (21.2%) of Gazprom's non-core business activities are devoted to social partnerships involving the operation of place-centered enterprises of various kinds, including (besides those already mentioned), a sewing plant, a potato processing plant, a chicken farm, and a porcelain factory.[15] By engaging in such social partnerships as building homes, constructing roads and sport centers, Gazprom fulfills the role not only of providing much needed jobs, but also of furthering the social welfare of the many communities in which it operates. In addition, by diversifying its operations, the company becomes more profitable.

An excellent demonstration of Gazprom's commitment to social partnerships is provided in Novy-Urengoy, the largest city in the Nadym-Pur-Taz region of northwest Siberia where most everyone works in Gazprom's nearby natural gas fields. Here, gas field technicians make up to $3,000 a month (the average Russian worker, by comparison, takes home $350 a month). The workers of Novy-Urengoy live with their families "in apartment blocks painted shades of blue, pink and yellow. Gazprom covers 97 percent of the cost of running 14 kindergartens, charging employees only 100 rubles, or $4 a month for child care. It provides interest-free loans, free medical care, and highly subsidized overseas vacations."[16] "Outside it can be -40 or -50 [but] [w]e work," comments one worker. "'Pride of the Nation,' [w]orking for Gazprom is considered prestigious." Though the state socialism of the former Soviet Union is gone, Gazprom's commitment to social partnerships undoubtedly "softens the rigors" of life in a region like Novy-Urengoy, referred to by locals simply as, "the North."[17]

Besides maintaining social partnerships, Gazprom also operates in many areas outside its main business. In 2005, the $13 billion acquisition of oil company Sibneft made Gazprom Russia's number five oil producer with 7 billion barrels of reserves. It owns Gazprombank (Russia's third largest bank), press and television outlets, including NTV, the only non fully state-owned major national channel. In 2004, Gazprom spent $2 billion to acquire 10 percent of the national electricity concern UES, and 25 percent of Mosenergo. Gazprom is also one of Russia's largest landowners through its ownership of dozens of former state and collective farms via local subsidiaries. It owns Sogas, Russia's fourth largest insurance company and has acquired a majority stake in Atom-Stroiexport, Russia's only exporter of nuclear power. It has also acquired a majority of OMZ, one of Russia's heavy machine enterprises. In addition, Gazprom owns 51 percent of Sibur, Russia's largest petrochemicals company. Gazpromavia, its in-house corporate airline, with a fleet of 108 aircraft, is among Russia's largest domestic airlines. Gazprom even has a football (soccer) team, the Zenit St. Petersburg, which it acquired in 2005, and is currently financing the construction of a new $200 million stadium to house it.[18]

To many Westerners, Europe's growing dependence on Gazprom and the natural gas it provides, gives Russia more leverage over Western Europe than some think it ought to have. Gazprom's swagger, displayed when, in January 2006, it temporarily cut gas flow to Ukraine, "and later [when Putin] intimated it might shift resources from Europe to China—reflects," write Jason Bush and Anthony Bianco of *Business Week*, "more than the company's muscle abroad." Gazprom's "assertiveness" at the center of Russia's foreign policy, also "points [both] to [its] ascendancy as Russia's preeminent economic institution" and as a central player in Russia's reformed economy.[19]

Gazprom is not Russia's only giant transnational. Lukoil, Russia's other petroleum giant, like Gazprom, has also expanded into the international market, opening its first line of gas stations in Poland in August 1996. Lukoil, which imports oil from the Kaliningrad enclave (the "fourth Baltic state"), which borders Poland and Lithuania, has plans to process about 500,000 tons of crude oil from Kaliningrad's Baltic shelf into gasoline. Between 1996 and 2001, Lukoil constructed about 200 gas stations in Poland.[20]

Since it was privatized as a public joint-stock company in April 1993, Lukoil, has become an increasingly powerful player in the volatile Trans-Caucasus, where its Baku-born president, Vagit Alekperov, acquired lucrative contracts by skillfully parlaying his local contacts. Lukoil was given added muscle in concluding deals due to the Russian government's virtual choke-hold on the region's pipelines. Together with Amoco and British Petroleum (BP), Lukoil acquired a 10 percent share of an international consortium to develop the Azeri, Chirag, and Gyuneshli fields and has a stake in four other projects in Azerbaijan and Kazakhstan, Russia's partners in the Commonwealth of Independent States (CIS), both of which, writes John Thornhill, "are reckoned to be among the most promising markets in the [twenty-first] century."[21]

Lukoil has also formed a joint-venture with Atlantic-Richfield, a U.S. oil group. In the coming years, both companies plan to invest $5 billion developing reserves in the Caspian Sea where production costs are lower and transportation easier than in Western Siberia. In North Africa, Lukoil joined up with the Italian oil company Agip, to develop fields in Tunisia, Libya and Egypt, while half way across the globe in Vietnam, Lukoil has sought a similar arrangement with the U.S. Penzoil group to exploit opportunities in that country.[22] Lukoil has even succeeded in expanding into the lucrative U.S. market. In the summer or 1997, Lukoil bought-out Getty oil to become America's newest gas retailer with the opening outside Washington D.C. of the first Russian filling-station. Located in Altavista, Virginia, the Lukoil station was the first of 2,000 filling-stations Lukoil constructed along the eastern coast of the U.S. by 2002, demonstrating that the Russian oil producer is, as a spokesperson for Lukoil commented, a "truly international company." As Lukoil president Vagit Alekperov commented, "This is an historic event. Never before has a Russian company done this. This allows Lukoil and Russia as a whole to strengthen their position in the American market." Alexei Kokiu, an analyst with Renaissance Capital, although cautioning that Lukoil had embarked on "a risky project in a tough market," nonetheless admitted that Lukoil had found a convenient niche in the American market which it succeeded in filling, namely, by providing its customers with one-stop shopping in the parking lots of U.S. food chains where its service stations are placed. The Alivista station is located in the parking lot of a Food Lion supermarket. Three other food chains, Richfords, Shaws Supermarkets, and Supervalue, also agreed to let Lukoil construct filling stations on their premises.[23]

One of Russia's most socially conscious Strategic Enterprises is Surgutneftgas, currently Russia's fourth largest oil producer.[24] Headquartered at Surgut in the Tyumen Oblast in Western Siberia, some 1500 miles from Moscow, Surgutneftgas has become, since its conversion to a worker-owned company in 1992, in terms of its total reserves, Russia's sixth largest vertically-integrated oil company with 11 percent of Russia's total oil output. At the time of its privatization, the state gave the preferred shares to Surgutneftgas' workers complete with a big dividend payment. Rank-and-file workers today own about 30 percent of the company, while managers own the remainder. The company's charter mandates that preferred shareholders (managers and rank-and-file workers), receive 20 percent of the net profits as dividends. In 2001, the company paid dividends to its workers on a net profit of $692 million—a figure some analysts feel vastly underestimates Surgutneftgas' actual net profits which have been put at somewhere around $2.66 billion.[25]

To compensate for extreme living conditions where winter temperatures can fall to -50°C, salaries are subsidized by the company. Moreover, the subsidy extends to all workers in Surgut, not just to those employed by the company. "By law," states Alkina Tsykyma, head of the Surgut office of the Oil and Gas Workers' Union, "all salaries [in Surgut] are increased by 120 percent over what they would be in temperate regions, in effect more than doubling them"—a clear demonstration of the social partnership Surgutneftgas maintains not only with its workers but with the community at large.[26]

Surgutneftgas accounts for more than 10 percent of Russia's total oil exports. In 1999, it began construction of its own port on the Baltic, near St. Petersburg on the Gulf of Finland. Its major refinery is located in the city of Kirishi in the Leningrad Oblast not far from St. Petersburg where Surgutneftgas controls wholesale and retail gasoline markets.[27]

Minority investors have accused Surgutneftgas of poor corporate transparency and bad management, prompting investment analyst Alexander Elder to comment: "[Surgutneftgas] is rich and secretive and nationalistic; it likes to keep foreigners out [by prohibiting] foreign holders from owning more than 5 percent of its shares…Its charismatic chairman, Vladimir Bogdanov, a man under 50, born in a local village, with an oil degree…still lives with his wife in an ordinary apartment and walks to work…."[28]

The Kremlin, on the other hand, considers Surgutneftgas one of its most favored companies. Putin has praised it for its socially responsible attitudes which include not only good pay for workers, but its willingness to invest in the local economy, demonstrating that, like Gazprom and other Russian worker-owned companies, Surgutneftgas as a place-centered company also maintains a firm commitment to social partnerships.[29]

Strategic Enterprises are appearing in other areas of economic activity besides the oil and gas sector, as the Kremlin tightens its control over the country's "natural monopolies." In April 2006, Russian officials announced plans to consolidate the airline industry by creating a dominant airline carrier through the transfer of several state-owned airlines into OAO Aeroflot. "It would be the latest in a series of Kremlin moves to consolidate prime assets under state control," writes reporter Guy Chazan.[30] Currently, the Russian government owns or has a stake in 188 mostly small airlines. Restoring "Aeroflot's Soviet-era monopoly on domestic routes," Chagin continues, comes "with the Russian state embarked on a wave of de facto nationalizations in strategic industries," including not only airlines, but also metals, aerospace and automobiles. In late 2005, Rosoboronexport announced that it was "seeking a stake in VSMPO-Avisma, one of the world's largest titanium producers and a major supplier to Western aircraft makers," including Airbus and Boeing. Under the proposal, VSMPO-Avisma would become part of a gigantic new state-owned company producing metals and alloys for Russia's defense industry.[31]

Boris Alyoshin, the head of Russia's Federal Industry Agency informed Chazin in an interview, "that he foresees the amalgamation of three of Russia's biggest automakers into a singe state holding company." It was "inevitable," Alyoshin declared, "that Avtovaz," recently acquired by the Russian state arms-trading agency Rosoboronexport, "would merge with Russian automaker GAZ, currently owned by Russian metals tycoon, Oleg Deripaska." He added that "[t]hey might be later joined by Kamaz, a big truck maker." Alyoshin was careful to stress that "any merged auto company would be privately owned," although, comments Chazin, "most observers assume that it will be controlled by the state."[32]

The Avtovaz take-over by Rosoboronexport, headed by Putin protégé, Sergei Chemezov, is the most recent example of Kremlin capitalism on the march. According to reporter Guy Chazan, "Chemezov has been using his [access to Putin] to turn the state agency...into a conglomerate with interests ranging from helicopters to oil-drilling gear to cars." Under Chemezov, Russian weapons exports boomed; in 2005, they totaled $6 billion, up 70 percent since 1999. That year also witnessed the state agency's merger "of all of Russia's helicopter-makers, some of them privately-owned, into one of its subsidiaries."

At the time of Rosoboronexport's take-over, Avtovaz was being threatened by corporate raiders, some allegedly with criminal connections. In response, Putin stepped in forcing Avtovaz's chief, 64-year-old Vladimir Kalannikov to retire, along with his entire staff, and the car-maker was subsequently placed under Rosoboronexport's control. In late December, 2005, Avtovaz's shareholders in Togliatti (the city where Avtovaz is located), elected a new board of directors who began by "pushing for $4.5 billion in state money to roll out new models and build a new factory to make 450,000 cars a year." To restore Avtovaz's "onetime glory" in the Russian auto industry, Chemezov announced it will build "a Jeep-type vehicle for the army to be called the Kalashnikov."

Rosoboronexport's take-over of Avtovaz also involved the state agency in a heated quarrel with U.S. auto-maker, General Motors, Avtovaz's joint-venture partner at the time. GM was shocked when, in February 2006, "the new bosses at Avtovaz suddenly stopped supplying parts...closing down its production line for 10 days." Following some tough negotiations, a compromise was reached that increased the price of parts Avtovaz supplied GM. Although GM claims that it remains committed to the joint-venture with Avtovaz, Vladimir Artyakov, Avtovaz's new chairperson, predicts that [Avtovaz] "might seek to buy out GM."

By curious coincidence, six months later, in late July 2006, the U.S. announced that it was imposing a two-year ban on Rosoboronexport, together with six other foreign companies, "for providing Iran with materials that could be used to make unconventional weapons or cruise or ballistic missile systems..." Also included under the July sanctions, which bar U.S. government agencies both from buying goods or services or providing them assistance, was the Russian aircraft maker, Sukhoi. Russia's Foreign Ministry responded by calling the sanction "unacceptable and denying that [Russia's] military trade with Iran had violated international laws." In 2005, Russia and Iran had signed an agreement which had involved the shipment of $1 billion in weapons, including the sale of TOR-M1 air defense missiles, although, according to Russian news reports at the time, "the deal had not yet been completed."[33]

As the driving force behind attempts by the Federal government to consolidate Russia's industrial assets, Boris Alyoshin has also spearheaded the creation of United Aircraft Corporation, "which will combine several of Russia's aerospace companies, some government-owned, some private, under state control."[34]

The United Aircraft Corporation emerged from new guidelines approved by Putin shortly after he took office. Dubbed, "Reform and Development of the Military-Industrial Complex, 2002-2006," the goal was "to aggregate 316 aerospace and defense enterprises into a dozen large firms specializing in aircraft engines, avionics, and other aerospace products." Douglas Barrie and Alexey Komarov of *Aviation Week and Space Technology*, in 2003, were informed by an industry executive that "Alyoshin believes we should take the private and state sectors and put them together, and he's got...Putin's support....It's the first time [the state and private sectors] have come to the same conclusion." The new corporation (UAC-OAK), "would include Sukhoi, MIG, Tupolev, Ilyushin, and Yakovlev (Russia's aircraft giants), along with Irkut, one of the few privatized airframe builders, also would be part of UAC-OAK."[35]

The appearance of the Strategic Enterprise encompassing most of Russia's "blue-chip" companies reflects a general trend in Russia toward greater state control of the economy. By 2004, a major shift in Putin's policy toward the business sector had taken place, provoked, no doubt, by the controversy over Mikhail Khodorkovsky.[36] After the hectic 1990s, which witnessed not only the sudden, unexpected demise of the Soviet Union and the command system, but the hiving-off of highly valuable economic assets during the infamous "loans-for-shares" scheme in 1994-1995, Putin, rather than renationalizing industries outright, sought their recovery with an increased measure of state control. After the scandal-ridden 1990s, it is apparent that Moscow may now want a greater say in how Russia's most valuable assets are to be disposed of in the future.[37] Under Putin's direction, the state had become one of the several forces driving economic change. As a result of his reelection in 2004 with a large majority and his overwhelming popularity with the Russian people, Putin headed a government which demanded that the state play a larger role both in the economy and in increased funding for social programs intended to raise living standards.[38] In this regard, both the Peoples' Enterprise and the Strategic Enterprise have an important part to play. Like the smaller People's Enterprise, the larger, more comprehensive Strategic Enterprise (Gazprom being the best example), is also place-centered and rooted in a single community or region. Through its commitment to social partnerships, the Strategic Enterprise makes its own contribution to community stability and social welfare. There can be little doubt that a significant reason for Russia's continuous economic growth since the dawn of the new millennium has chiefly been due to the success of both the People's Enterprise and the Strategic Enterprise in helping to drive the Russian economy.

Notes

1. John Thornhill, "Here Come the Russian Multinationals," *Russia Review*, 2 December 1996, p. 10.
2. Ibid.
3. Ibid. See also, Mark Mobius, with Stephen Fenichell, *Passports to Profits: Why the Next Investment Windfalls Will be Found Abroad—and How to Grab Your Share* (New York: Warner Books, 1999), 105-160. Mobius' predictions were realized when, in November 2003, Severstal, the Russian steel giant, gained the right to purchase Rouge Industries, Inc., the steelmaking operation located at the historic Rouge industrial complex in Dearborn, Michigan. Built in 1920 by Henry Ford "the Rouge plant," comments reporter Jeff Bennett, "grew to become an American symbol of the power of manufacturing and the strength of the [U.S.] car industry." Competition by foreign imports and consolidation within the steel industry, forced the Rouge to file for bankruptcy in October 2003 after it had posted combined losses of $360.3 million since 1999. On November 24, 2003, turning aside a challenge by the U.S. Steel Corp., a Delaware federal bankruptcy court approved Severstal's bid to buy the company for $215 million, making the Rouge the first Russian-owned steel plant in the United States. In late January 2004, the Rouge's 2,600 workers ratified a labor contract that cut 400 jobs but provided that Severstal pay health-care costs for current employees and left hourly wages largely intact. Mike Hudson, "U.S. Steel May Try to Buy Rouge," *Detroit News*, 28 October 2003, pp. B1, B8; Jeff Bennett, "Steel Deal Signed, Fought," *Detroit Free Press*, 22 November 2003, pp. 13A, 14A; Jeff Bennett, "Symbol of U.S. Strength, Weakness," *Detroit Free Press*, 24 November 2003, p. B8; Jeff Bennett, "Rouge Assets Up for Grabs by Suitors," *Detroit Free Press*, pp. 1C, 2C; Mike Hudson, "Court approves Sale of Rouge Steel," *Detroit News*, p. 1C; "Workers Ratify Rouge Steel Pact," (Metro Business), *Detroit News*, 30 January 2004, p. 2B.

The rise of multinational companies, like Severstal, from emerging economies is also leading to a shift in economic power as these companies continue to purchase businesses in both rich and poor countries alike. "Economic theory," declares *The Economist*, "says that this should not happen. Richer countries should export capital to poorer ones, not the other way round. Economists have had to get used to seeing this turned on its head in recent years" as rich countries with large current accounts deficits borrow from poorer emerging economies (like China) with large surpluses. Similarly, foreign direct investment (FDI)—the buying of companies and the building of factories and offices abroad—should also flow from rich to poor and with it managerial and entrepreneurial prowess." Moreover, emerging-market multinationals, instead of just buying Western know-how, have been bringing technological and managerial skill, as well as money, to the companies they purchase. Severstal's Russian workers are not only exchanging ideas with colleagues in the U.S. on improving techniques in steelmaking. According to Chris Kristock, head of advanced engineering at Severstal-Detroit, American engineers "have also picked up useful technical tips on automotive steel from their Russian colleagues," who, in the past, were helped "in a series of technological exchanges involving Arcelor of Luxembourg (Now Arcelor-Mittal), and Japan's Nippon Steel, two of the world's most advanced steelmakers." Russian steelmakers, we are told, "are also experts at revitalizing run-down plants like the Rouge and Oregon Mills," another U.S. steel plant purchased by Severstal. At the Magnitogorsk Iron and Steelworks (MMK) in the city of Magnitogorsk on the slopes of the Ural Mountains, MMK, "[o]nce the archetypal Soviet dinosaur,...over the past decade [1997-2007], has spent $2.6 billion to replace its ancient, polluting blast furnaces with state-of-the-art smelting equipment." Severstal's newest plant, under construction in Mississippi (SeverCorr), "will be the first to use an electric furnace for automotive steel, a less labor-intensive—and more cost-effective—technology." Globalization, to its critics, "may be little more than a license for giant Western companies to colonize the emerging world," states *The Economist*. "[Y]et [as Russia's Severstal has shown], more and more firms from poorer economies are planting their flags in rich ground." See, "Wind of Change," and "The Challengers," *The Economist*, 12 January 2008, pp. 12, 13, 62-64. Also, Jason Bush, "Russia's Steel Mills Roll into America," *Business Week*, 1 October 2007, p. 44; articles by Peter Marsh, "Severstal Plans $1 billion Investment in the U.S.;" "Détente Between Steelmakers Part of Russian Industrial Revolution," *Financial Times*, 31 December 2007, p. 16.

4. Thane Gustafson, *Capitalism: Russian Style* (Cambridge: University Press, 1997), 54.

5. Ibid.

6. Alexander Gubsky, "Gazprom: Russia's Brightest Burning Star," *Russia Review*, 9 September 1996, pp. 26, 27.

7. John Lloyd, *Birth of a Nation: An Anatomy of Russia* (London: Michael Joseph, 1998), 278.

8. Ibid., 178, 181; also *Business Week*, 7 June 2004, p. 58.

9. Thornhill, "Here Come the Russian Multinationals," p. 10.

10. Neil Buckley, "Comment Analysis," *Financial Times*, 15 April 2005, p. 13.

11. Ibid.

12. Ibid.

13. Andrew E. Kramer, Steven Lee Myers, "Workers' Paradise is Rebranded as Kremlin Inc.," *New York Times*, 24 April 2006, pp. A1, A10.

14. Lloyd, *Rebirth of a Nation*, 278; also, Piveronus, *The Reinvention of Capitalism*, Chapter 6.

15. Alexander Elder, *Rubles to Dollars: Making Money on Russia's Exploding Financial Frontier* (New York: New York Institutes of Finance, 1999), 179, 180; also, Kramer and Myers, "Workers' Paradise is Rebranded as Kremlin, Inc.," p. A10.

16. Jason Bush and Anthony Bianco, "Why Russians Love Gazprom—No Matter What the World Thinks," *Business Week*, 31 July 2006, pp. 36, 37.

17. Ibid.

18. Ibid., pp. 38, 39.

19. Ibid.

20. Thornhill, "Here Come the Russian Multinationals," p. 11; also Reuters, "In Brief," *Russia Review*, 9 September 1996, p. 27. Lukoil, a public joint-stock company, in 1995, produced 1.1 million barrels of oil per day. "On paper at least," write Daniel Yergin and Thane Gustafson, Lukoil is "potentially one of the largest oil companies in the

world in terms of production." Indeed, "within a matter of years," Lukoil could become "a major force in the world oil industry," if it has not already done so. Daniel Yergin and Thane Gustafson, *Russia 2010: and What it Means for the World* (New York: Vintage Books, 1995), 282.

21. Thornhill, "Here Come the Russian Multinationals," pp. 9, 11.

22. Ibid.

23. Jeanne Whalen, "Russia Invades the American Market," *Russia Review*, 25 August 1997, p. 24.

24. David Hoffman, "The Oligarch Who Came in From the Cold," *Forbes*, 18 March 2002. The Russian State Committee for Geology estimates Surgutneftgas's oil reserves at 11.1 billion barrels. Surgutneftgas pegs them at 22 billion barrels. According to the Ministry of Fuel and Energy, Surgutneftgas has enough reserves to last 42 years at the current rate of production. Elder, *Rubles to Dollars*, 175-181.

25. Jeanne Whalen, "Russian Oil Firm Thrives and Investors Are Fed Up With It," *Wall Street Journal*, 8 May 2001, p. A21.

26. Eric Helque, "Boom Times: Siberia's Oil-Rich Middle Class," *Russian Life* (May/June 2004), pp. 56-62.

27. Elder, *Rubles to Dollars*, 175-181.

28. Ibid.

29. Neil Buckley, "Comment Analysis," p. 13.

30. Guy Chazan, "Russia May Rebuild Aeroflot Into National Carrier," *New York Times*, 24 April 2006, p. A2.

31. Ibid.

32. Guy Chazan, "Russian Car Maker Comes Under Sway of Old Pal of Putin," *Wall Street Journal*, 19 May 2006, pp. A1, A7; Helene Cooper, "U.S. Puts Sanctions on Seven Foreign Companies Dealing with Iran," *New York Times*, 5 August 2006, p. A3.

33. Ibid.

34. Ibid.

35. Alexey Komarov and Michael Taverna, "Russia, Inc.," *Aviation Week & Space Technology*, 11 August 2003, p. 53; Douglas Barrie and Alexey Komarov, "Emergency Situation," *Aviation Week & Space Technology*, 8 December 2003, p. 36.

36. The Khodorkovsky affair, so called, is discussed in detail in my earlier book, *The Reinvention of Capitalism*, 113-115.

37. Russia is not alone in protecting its strategic sectors from foreign takeovers. In August 2005, the French Industry Minister, Francois Loos, in an interview with the French newspaper, *Les Echos*, announced that the French government will publish a list of strategic sectors that it wants to keep in French hands. These include the transport, pharmaceutical, biotech, electronics and energy sectors. In 2004, former Prime Minister, Jena-Pierre Raffrain, told reporter, Jo Wrighton, that France's government, "would oppose any foreign takeovers of companies in these industries." Jo Wrighton, "France to Protect Strategic Sectors from Foreign Deals," *Wall Street Journal*, 20 August 2005, p. A3.

38. Russia's booming economy has enabled the Federal government in Moscow to pour huge sums into long-neglected social programs, initiating what *Business Week* reporter, Jason Bush, labels as "Russia's New Deal." In 2006, Federal tax revenues rose to $240 billion, while economic growth since 1999, the year Putin took office, has averaged 6.8 percent annually. Health, education, housing and agriculture have all benefited from the state's largesse. In health care, pay for family doctors has doubled to an average of $750 per month. To encourage population growth, new mothers receive grants of $270 for prenatal and child care. In education, by the end of 2007, the government expects to

provide high-speed Internet to all of Russia's 60,000 schools, 3,000 of which will receive million-ruble grants for technology. Russia's 10,000 best teachers (out of a total of 1.5 million), will receive awards of $3,800 each in addition to their monthly salary which has averaged only $260 nationally. Apartment and home builders will receive loan guarantees and subsidies. A state-supported mortgage agency, to encourage home loans, will pay up to 40 percent of the cost of new homes for young families. In agriculture, the state will provide funding for interest payments on loans to small farms and subsidize up to 70 percent of housing costs for 30,000 farmers. To help fund these programs, $300 million has been earmarked in new capital for the creation of a state agricultural bank. Jason Bush, "Russia's New Deal, *Business Week*, 9 April 2007, pp. 40-45.

Chapter Four

Eurasianism: The Mackinder Thesis Revisited

Eurasianism grew out of the search for what Dostoyevsky called "the Russian idea." Since the early years of the nineteenth-century, Russia's search for a national identity has preoccupied and divided Russian intellectuals. The publication, in 1836, of Pytr Chaadayev's scandalous "First Philosophical Letter" split Russia's intelligentsia into two mutually opposing camps, Slavophiles and Westernizers. In contrast to the Westernizers who saw Russia's destiny tied to the West, Chaadayev insisted "that Russia was a land apart, a 'unique civilization'...the result of our never having walked side by side with other nations...We belong to none of the great families of mankind; we are neither of the West nor of the East.'"[1]

Slavophiles and Westernizers both of whom had their roots in the 1812 war against Napoleon's invasion of Russia, initially emerged in the 1830s. "The horrors of the French Revolution," writes cultural historian Orlando Figis, "had led the Slavophiles to reject the universal culture of the Enlightenment and to emphasize instead those indigenous traditions that distinguished Russia from the West." In the aftermath of the failed Decemberist revolt of 1825 for a constitutional monarch, Russian intellectuals began to search for a more "Russian" way. This led Slavophiles to look "first to the virtues they discerned in the patriarchal customs of the countryside....They idealized the common folk (*narod*) as the true bearer of the national character (*narodnost*)....As devout upholders of the Orthodox ideal, they maintained that the Russian was defined by Christian sacrifice and humility. This was the foundation of the spiritual community (*sabornost*) in which, they imagined, the squire and the serf were bound together by their patriarchal customs and Orthodox beliefs."[2]

Westernizers, by way of contrast, embraced the West and saw Russia's destiny tied to Europe. One of their leading spokespersons in the 1830s and 1840s was Alexander Herzen. Like his fellow contemporary, Chaadayev, Herzen, writes Wesleyan University professor, Philip Pomper, "pictured Russia as a young, vigorous and promising nation which might contribute to the general progress of mankind." Instead of Orthodox Christianity, Herzen's universal principle was socialism based on the "populist belief that the Russian masses possessed unique socialist and revolutionary attributes not unrelated to the Slavophile vision of the spiritually superior Orthodox peasantry." Like the Slavophiles, Herzen also rejected what he considered the decadence of the West. "Since Europe seemed unable to tear herself free from her medieval past, Herzen," continues Professor Pomper, "believed that youthful Russia might actually arrive at socialism first, skipping the decadent phase of bourgeois civilization." Following the violent suppression of the worker's insurrection in Paris in 1848, Herzen embraced radicalism and was converted temporarily into a "revolutionary anarchist with nationalistic bias. The Russian peasant commune became the object upon which Herzen projected his longings for an anarchistic variety of socialism."[3]

In recent years, particularly after the disintegration of the Soviet Union, the Slavophile-Westernizer debate has reignited and out of it, writes the Russian scholar, Ilya Vinkovetsky, Eurasianism "emerged as an object of popular and scholarly fascination...." The downfall of the Soviet Union, he adds, "has not only prompted, but forced, its former citizens to redefine their identities, and it so happens that Eurasianism, openly discussed for the first time after years of suppression, seems to provide answers to many of their questions." It is no coincidence, as Vinkovetsky adds in a footnote, that "the increase in the popular appeal of Eurasianism has paralleled the growing popular distrust for what are commonly understood to be Western prescriptions to Russia's problems and the growing nostalgia for some aspects of the old Soviet Union."[4] We should also add that the current debate over which direction Russia's economic reforms should take and how fast, or slow, they should arrive, is complimentary to the growing appeal of Eurasianism. "Russia's current turbulent times have prompted the country's citizens to seek new signposts." What was, Vinkovetsky continues, "a feeling of great disorientation and bitter disillusionment with the fate of their country and the signposts of the past" following the Bolshevik Revolution of 1917, has, in the aftermath of the Soviet Union's sudden demise, prompted, like then, a "radically new vision" of Russia's identity.[5]

Eurasianism originated from the theory of geopolitics, popularized at the start of the twentieth-century by Scottish geographer, Sir Halford Mackinder.[6] At the time, geopolitics constituted a new branch of the social sciences that combined the principles of geography and politics in order to study the distribution of political power worldwide. To the geopoliticians of the period, the entire world represented a vast arena of competition in which the great powers of the day (Great Britain, France, Germany, Russia, Japan and the United States), struggled for control of economically valuable resources, territory and population. The entire land mass of Europe, extending from Spain to Siberia, constituted a vast terrain of land, raw materials and people, the control of which, or so it was believed, would decide the outcome of what the followers of geopolitics saw as the forthcoming contest for world domination.[7]

In January 1904, in London, Mackinder presented a paper before the Royal Geographical Society titled, "The Geographical Pivot of History."[8] Some months later, the paper was published in the prestigious *Geographical Journal*, along with a transcript of the discussion that followed. Mackinder's lecture, writes Michigan State University Distinguished Professor of Geography, Harm de Blij, "raised a storm of reaction and for decades afterward was the most cited article in geography."[9]

According to Mackinder, geopolitics posits that the earth is divided into two mutually antagonistic spheres or regions—the "world island" which consists of the land-linked continents of Europe, Asia and Africa—and arrayed along its periphery, the large "insular groups," the Americas (North and South), Australia and New Zealand, Japan and the British Isles. Of the two, the "world island" is the largest, most populous and richest in terms of natural resources. At the center of the "world island" is what Mackinder designated, the Eurasian "heartland," or "pivot area," the stretch of territory that lay in Eastern Europe and Western Russia.[10] In the past, periodic invasions along the "pivot area" (Napoleon's invasion of Russia in 1812 being a good example), had failed to establish permanent control of the "heartland" mainly because of the inability of invading armies to assure continual supplies of men and material.

In the late nineteenth-century, however, the revolution in transportation brought about by the railroad, abolished for all practical purpose, the seeming invulnerability of the "heartland" to domination by a single power, and made penetration into the "heartland" by a powerful, continental power possible. "Who rules east Europe commands the 'heartland,'" declared Mackinder, "[w]ho rules the 'heartland' commands the 'world island;' who rules the world island commands the world."[11] This was the geopolitical nightmare that was to haunt the world's two major sea powers—the United State and Great Britain—during most of the twentieth-century. The nightmare that Mackinder identified in 1904 was the prospect that the conquest of Eastern Europe either by Germany or Russia (Europe's two great land powers), would lead to the domination of the Eurasian landmass by one or both of them as a prelude to mastery of the world.

Mackinder's 1904 article received a great deal of attention following World War II when the Soviet Union, representing the "world island" along with its ally Communist China, emerged as one of the world's two superpowers. The "insular groups," represented by the United States and its NATO allies (Great Britain included), stood in armed opposition, provoking the Cold War which lasted until the dissolution of the Soviet Union in 1991. The overriding fear at the time, was that with the Soviet Union and China dominating much of the "world island," Communism would, unless "contained," ultimately exercise mastery of the whole world. After 1991, with the Soviet colossus gone, the "heartland," albeit for different reasons, has, once again, become the focus of attention.[12]

Eurasianism in Russia is directly descended from the Slavophile movement of the nineteenth-century. Born in 1921 among the scattered émigrés who fled Soviet Russia following the Bolshevik Revolution and Civil War, it first found expression in historian Peter Savitsky's *Exodus to the East*, described as "a collection of ten essays published in Sofia [Bulgaria], in which Eurasianists foresaw the West's destruction and the rise of a new civilization led by Russia or Eurasia."[13] Rather than stressing the cultural union of all Slavs (as did the Slavophiles prior to the Polish uprisings of the 1860s), modern-day Eurasianism "looks south and east and dreams of fusing Eurasia's Orthodox and Muslim population into one."[14] According to the author of the most important essay in the collection, Nikolai S. Trubetskoi, Russia is "a steppland Asian culture."[15] Given that the Slavic element "was undoubtedly of fundamental importance in the formation of Russian nationality," Russian folk culture, Trubetskoi emphasizes, "had developed more through contact with the East."[16] A contemporary version of this theme was advanced by Vadim Tsymbursky who, as James Billington informs us, has proposed "a new Eurasian 'ethnogenesis' which results from an amalgam of 'the plowman' and 'the horseman:' the sedentary but virtuous Slavic peasantry with nomadic but daring 'Turanian' [Mongolian and Turkic peoples of Asian Russia]." Combined into "a new superethos, they could [then] resist 'the globalist temptation' offered by the only remaining superpower [and] build a new and better civilization in unspoiled Eurasia."[17]

Asian influence, as Trubetskoi points out, was paramount and made evident in several ways, in music, dancing, psychology, but especially in language. Proto-Slavic, the progenitor of all the Slavic languages, and those dialects closely associated with it, the Baltic dialects (Lithuanian, Latvian and Old Prussian), "owing to [their] central position" among the Proto-Indo-European languages, "exhibit detailed similarities in the area of...'little words' (so characteristic of and important to every language)," with Proto-Indo-Iranian dialects of the East. "This allows us to assume," proclaims Trubetskoi, "an especially close bond between the Proto-Slavic and Proto-Iranian dialects."[18]

Close linguistic ties between Slavic and Iranian are also especially evident in religion. The Indo-European word, *deiwos*, "which means 'god' in other languages," Trubetskoi informs us, "in the Slavic and Iranian languages denotes an evil mythological being..." In reference to the Iranians, this semantic change "is usually explained by the reform of Zarathustra (Zoroaster) who recognized Ahura Mazdah (Ormazd) as the one true god and then declared all other gods to be demons; consequently, the term *daeva* came to mean 'demon' while 'god' was denoted by other words (among them *baga* [both Slavic and Old Iranian world for 'god'])." Concluding, Trubetskoi declares, "[o]ne must assume that the ancestors of the Slavs participated in some way in the evolution of religious ideas which ultimately lead to Zarathustra's reform among their eastern neighbors, the ancient Iranians."[19] Thus, just as the Slavs were connected "physically" to the Western Indo-Europeans "owing to geographical circumstances, 'spiritually' they 'were drawn to the Indo-Iranians....'"[20]

From an ethnographic standpoint, if we are to trust Trubetskoi's judgment, "the Russian people are not purely Slavic." Down through the centuries, "the Russians freely intermingled with the Finno-Ugric tribes, the Mongolians and other nomad peoples from the steppe. They had assimilated elements of their languages, their music, customs and religion, so that these Asiatic cultures had become absorbed in Russia's own historical evolution."[21] Taken together, they comprise what Trubetskoi labels the "Turanian East," a connection which "has not only an ethnographic but an anthropological basis: Turkic blood mingles in Russian veins with that of the Ugro-Finns and Slavs. And the Russian national character is unquestionably linked in certain ways with the 'Turanian East.'"[22]

Today, Eurasianism, we are told, "has become the common focus of Russia's 'red-brown' coalition—the alliance of ultra-left and ultra-right politicians who together [in 2000 controlled] close to half of the Duma (Russia's lower house of parliament)...."[23] Essentially, Eurasianism emphasizes Russia's uniqueness and argues that Russia does not need to adopt Western (particularly American) political and economic models in order to succeed as a modern nation. Hard-line Eurasianists envision a Eurasian "heartland" "as the geographic launch pad for a global anti-Western movement whose goal is the ultimate expulsion of 'Atlantic' influence from Eurasia." Followers of this school of thought include Gennadi Zyuganov, leader of the Russian Communist Party, Yevgeny Primakov, one-time Prime Minister to Boris Yeltsin, and Aleksandr Dugin, former deputy to Alexandr Prokhanov, editor of the opposition newspaper, *Zavtra* (Tomorrow).

In 1999, Zyuganov published *The Geography of Victory*, a geopolitical manifesto in which he abandons anything which resembles Marxist-Leninist dogma, and reinvents the Russian Communist Party by combining nationalism, religious orthodoxy, and Marxism.[24] James Billington describes Zyuganov as a "little known figure from the propaganda department of the Communist Central Committee," who, during the 1980s, "tried to forge a political alliance with extremist nationalist ideologues which had been promoted to prominence by the Brezhnev regime...." As such, Zyuganov represents, Billington goes on to say, "the first of many efforts to forge a left-right or 'red-brown' political bloc in opposition to liberalization." Unable to block Gorbachev's reforms or prevent the dissolution of the Soviet Union, "their coming together in 1990-91 pointed to the nationalist direction that Zyuganov, the then emerging new communist leader, would take in his continuing struggle against democratization in post-Soviet Russia."[25]

In order "to win the radical vote at both ends of the political spectrum," Zyuganov, writes Charles Clover in *Foreign Affairs*, outflanked the nationalists and succeeded in bridging the gap between White and Red in Russian society, "first by linking Russia's 'national idea' to popular traditions and Russian Orthodox Christianity, and then by folding these back into Communism." In his 1995 book, *Za Gorizontum* (Beyond the Horizon), Zyuganov "argues that the traditional Russian idea of *obshina* (community) and the Orthodox doctrine of *sobornost* (communitarianism)—both of which endorse collective property ownership and communal decision-making—reveal that communism has actually been a [major] theme in Russian society throughout history."[26]

As an Eurasianist, Zyuganov makes common cause not only with Russian nationalism; he is also a staunch supporter of the nationalist ambitions of Russia's myriad ethnic groups, including, among others, the Bashkirs, Tatars and Kalmyks. "Zyuganov's big idea," continues Clover, "is that all traditional societies are profoundly socialist ones. He has skillfully connected ethnic nationalism with communist notions of friendship between nationalities to sew all Eurasian ethnic groups together into an antiliberal, anti-Western patchwork of traditionalism and collectivism."[27] In Zyuganov's view, therefore, Communism and Russian-Eurasian tradition are one.

In his latest book, *The Geography of History*, Zyuganov attempts, "to correlate class struggle with East-West conflict." Declaring that Russia "will never be bourgeois," Zyuganov goes on to claim "that Russia has been subordinated by the West and has become a mere source of raw material—an unhappy predicament he considers analogous to the fate of the postcolonial East."[28] For Zyuganov, the "root of the conflict...lies in the very character of Western civilization"—the division of society into "haves" and "have-nots," a tradition, he points out, "which extends all the way back to ancient (democratic) Athens." According to Zyuganov, this split "is a fundamental tenet of the Western worldview: the 'Golden Billion' of the world's inhabitants living in the West," he declares, "are free from obligation toward the rest of humanity, and [the] remainder usefully and justly play their role of resource-supplying appendages, reservoirs of toxic waste, and spaces for placing ecologically harmful production."[29] In the battle against the "global class struggle," Russia, "must first consolidate the Orthodox world into a single bloc and forge close ties with radical Islam," which Zyuganov sees, as "the real alternative to the hegemony of Western civilization [and] return to the centuries-old national spiritual traditions [which] can lead the way to very positive results. It is the return to moral norms of relationships between people...keeping intact society's morals."[30]

Zyuganov also urges Russia, we are told, "to recover its 'national governmental self-awareness' and become 'the principal supporter of the Eurasian bloc against the hegemonic tendencies of the U.S.A. and the great Atlantic space.'" To accomplish this will require that Russia "reassert its 'ethnic commonality' with its 'mononational core of Great Russia, Little Russia [Ukraine] and Belarus,' which, in turn, has 'Eurasia as a superethos.'" Beyond this, Zyuganov envisions the eventual formation of "an even broader Eurasian power bloc" resulting from "an alliance among Russia, China and India."[31]

Taking center stage in the Eurasianist movement is Alexandr Dugin, currently editor of the journal *Elements: Eurasian Survey*, who had once worked as an advisor to the one-time Communist speaker of the Russian Duma, Gennadi Seleznev. Dugin came to the fore of the Eurasianist movement following the publication, in 1997, of his controversial book, *The Basics of Geopolitics: Russia's Geopolitical Future*, which he coauthored with the assistance of Russia's Military Academy of the General Staff.[32] The ideas in Dugin's book can be viewed as an updated version of the Mackinder thesis. Mackinder's idea of the geopolitical opposition between land and sea powers is taken one step further by Dugin who posits "that the two worlds are not just governed by competing strategic imperatives, but are fundamentally opposed to each other culturally." This land and sea antagonism "parallels the East-West divide. Land based societies," Dugin theorizes, "are attracted to absolute value systems and tradition, while maritime societies are inherently liberal."[33]

In strategic terms, Dugin proposes, "based on their shared rejection of the West...that an anti-Western alliance of Russia, Germany, and Iran...would be capable of expelling American influence from the continent." Coincidentally, Dugin's ideas "foreshadowed Yeltsin's call [in the late 1990s] for a Moscow-Berlin-Paris axis and Primakov's initiatives toward Iran and Iraq [which began while he was Yeltsin's foreign minister]."[34] According to Dugin, Russia should think of itself as "a new Eurasia empire" which would be able to mobilize the Eurasian continent "for a global struggle against 'Atlanticism.'" Rejecting the "mondialism" of "the rich north" (Western Europe and North America), Russia is to become the leader "in forging new 'axes' for anti-Atlantic agitation with Berlin, Tokyo and Iran. The key to success will be a 'Russo-Islamic pact.'" Russia, Dugin predicts, will eventually become the central component of a "Eurasian Union," "the lynchpin of a 'continental bloc' that will prevail over the Atlanticists.'"[35]

Like Dugan, most Eurasianists distinguish themselves from Russian nationalists "by advocating alliances with Russia's Asian neighbors, especially its Islamic ones."* Such is the view of Yevgeny Primakov, Russia's ranking Arabist and Asia specialist and one-time Russian Prime Minister. Since the early 1990s, we are told, Primakov "has been the driving force behind Russia's deepening relations with the pariah states of the Middle East, notably Iran and Iraq [before the fall of Saddam Hussein in 2003]." In his 1983 book, *The East After the Collapse of the Colonial System*, Primakov describes the manner by which the imperial West has attempted to exert its control over the post-colonial East through what he terms "asymmetrical independence," affirming the Soviet Union's historical role as the East's true guardian.[36]

Primakov's views in this respect are shared by A.S. Panarin, the head of the Institute of Philosophy of the Russian Academy of Sciences. In 1995, Panarin began to argue publicly "that Russia after the Cold War should play a role in Eurasia similar to that which the United States played in the North Atlantic world after World War II." Just as the U.S. had become "a new caesar for Western Europe," Russia "would play the ever more exalted role of the new Alexander the Great for Eurasia." Panarin's strategy envisions a "United States of Eurasia" emerging from a dialogue between Orthodox Christianity and Islam,

---

* A.S. Tuminez categorizes Russian nationalists today into four types—*liberal nativists*, who define Russia's mission as "primarily defensive and inward-looking: to restore and defend the physical and spiritual well-being of the land and people;" *Westernizing democrats* who regard Russia as "a great power whose immense potential can be realized through democracy, market reform, and integration and participation in the international community;" *statist nationalists* who reject communism and deplore the breakup of the Soviet Union by advocating a leading role for Russia and the CIS, and a foreign policy that "distinctly defends Russian national interest;" and *national patriots* comprised of "a variety of leftist and rightest views, including Stalinists and fascists, who generally want to see Russia restored to its former status as a great imperial power." A.S. Tuminez, "Nationalism and the Interest in Russian Foreign Policy," in C.A. Wallender, ed., *The Sources of Russian Foreign Policy after the Cold War Modern World* (Oxford. UK: Blackwell, 1999), 275.

both of which represent the world's "two great written traditions." Working in tandem, they would oppose "their common enemy: Western secularism and individualism." Emerging from "the Muslim-Orthodox dialogue will come a new type of 'continental thinking' that will reintegrate the republics of the former USSR culturally and provide a better developmental model for the post-modern world." Panarin also sees Russia as "an agent of 'the revenge of history' against the Western idea that democracy and a globalized economy heralded the 'end of history.' He plays with the idea of Russia linking up with India, Iran and China to counter the G-7 alliance of North America, Europe and Japan." In such a loose alliance, Russia, "would play a pivotal role."[37]

Both Primakov and Panarin, it seems, share the same Eurasianist strategy which, in Alexandr Dugin's view, consists of "left-wing economic policies at home, helping Arab states abroad, orientation toward the East, helping traditional friends like Serbia and strengthening the integration of the former Soviet Union. This is Eurasianism, the policy of the heartland." It may also be, concludes Clover, what he terms Russia's "third way, and may well represent the future of Russian foreign policy."[38]

Notes

1. Andrew Meier, *Black Earth: A Journey Through Russia After the Fall* (New York: W.W. Norton & Co., 2003), 338, 339. See also, Peter Yakovlovich Chaadayev, *Philosophical Letters & Apology of A Madman*, trans., Mary-Barbara Zeldin (Knoxville: University of Tennessee Press, 1969), 6. Chaadayev, we should add, was a close friend and protégé of Puskin who "declared that all of his own political ideas came from Chaadayev." (Meier, 339).

2. Orlando Figis, *Natasha's Dance: A Cultural History of Russia* (New York: Henry Holt & Co., 2002), 133, 134.

3. Philip Pomper, *The Russian Revolutionary Intelligentsia* (Arlington Heights, IL: Harlan Davidson, Inc., 1970), 42-44. According to Lesley Chamberlain, the difference between Westernizers and Slavophiles "was in their underlying philosophy of ethics in relation to knowledge. The Slavophiles were religious conservatives, the Westernizers, atheist progressives, which put them in separate camps with regard to science and reason….The Slavophiles…were skeptical of the civilizing power of reason." Be that as it may, their "differences in direction did not deter men in either camp from believing Russia's future was unique and lay apart." Lesley Chamberlain, *Motherland: A Philosophical History of Russia* (New York: Overlook Rookery, 2004, 2007), 46.

4. Ilya Vinkovetsky, "Eurasianism in Its Time: A Bibliography," in *Forebodings and Events: An Affirmation of the Eurasians*, trans. and ed., Ilya Vinkovetsky (Idyllwild, CA: Charles Schlacks, Jr., Publisher, 2003), 152, 24n. Originally published in Russian as, *Iskhod k Vostoku* (Sofiia: Tipografiia "Balkan" 1921).

5. Ibid., 155. Eurasianism is also viewed, observes James Billington, who labels it, "the authoritarian alternative," as Russia's answer to economic globalization, which was seen as undermining the unspoiled community-centered peoples of the Eurasian heartland with the vulgar consumerism, licentiousness, and selfish individualism of the West."

Billington, *Russia in Search of Itself*, 72. "The great originality of the Eurasians," writes noted Russian historian, Nicolas V. Riasanovsky, "consisted in the fact that they were the first Russian ideologues to separate Russia completely from its European moorings and fundamental connections." The "basic assertion" of Eurasianists is "that their country was not [just] Russia but Eurasia, quite distinct, for instance, from France or Japan, but a symbiotic organic unit bordering on the Pacific, the Himalayas, and Central Europe." Nicholas V. Riasanovsky, *Russian Identities: A Historical Study* (Oxford: University Press, 2005), 234.

6. William Keylor, *The Twentieth-Century World: An International History* (New York & Oxford: Oxford University Press, 1984), 29-33.

7. Ibid.

8. H.J. Mackinder, "The Geographical Pivot of History," *Geographical Journal*, 23 (1904): 421-437.

9. Harm de Blij, *Why Geography Matters: Three Challenges Facing America* (Oxford: University Press, 2005), 128.

10. Ibid.

11. Keylor, *The Twentieth-Century World*, 29-33.

12. Mackinder's leading American disciple was James Burnham, referred to by Karl E. Meyer and Shareen Blair Brysac as, "the most original thinking theoretician of the Cold War." Born in 1905 in Chicago, Burnham graduated summa cum laude from Princeton University in 1926. During the 1930s, Burnham was editor of the Trotskyite journal, *The New International*. In 1940, after breaking with Trotsky, Burnham published the book, *The Managerial Revolution*, whose supporters included George Orwell and John Kenneth Gailbraith. In 1945, while serving with the OSS, Burnham wrote in the *Partisan Review*, a much discussed essay on Stalin in which he embraced the Mackinder thesis, "together with his predilection for hypnotic capital letters, in identifying the source of Soviet power in 'the magnetic core of the Eurasian heartland,'" which "progresses outward through spheres of Adsorption, Domination, and Orienting Influence until dissipating beyond Eurasia in zones of 'momentary Appeasement and Infiltration (England, the United States).' In order to take on the Eurasian dragon...Americans had to assume Britain's global role...Americans were to be the 'receiver' for the disintegrating British Empire." In 1947, his book, *The Struggle for the World*, was published the same week that President Truman proclaimed the so called Truman Doctrine, in which he called on Congress to replace Britain in providing military assistance to Greece and Turkey. A twelve page essay in *Life* magazine focused on Burnham's "provocative thesis that World War III had already begun in Greece," calling on Americans "to mobilize the democratic world to challenge the Soviet empire." Karl E. Mayer and Shareen Blair Brysac, *The Tournament of Shadows: The Great Game and the Race for Empire in Central Asia* (New York: Basic Books, 1999), 568, 569.

During the final years of the Soviet Union, Eurasianism briefly came into vogue due, we are told, to the writings of Lev Gumilyov, the anthropologist son of St. Petersburg poets, Anna Akhmatova and Nikolai Gumilyov. Although Gumilyov's critics denounced his Eurasianism as a hidden form of nationalism with anti-Western, anti-Semitic undertones, his close friend, the St. Petersburg historian, Alexsandr Panchenko, who coauthored several works with him, defends his theory. Meier, *Black Earth*, 340. Also, Viktor Shnireman and Sergei Panarin, "Lev Gumilev: His Pretensions as a Founder of Ethnology and His Eurasian Theories," *Inner Asia* 3 (2001): 1-18.

13. Figes, *Natasha's Dance*, 423.

14. Clover, "Dreams of the Eurasian Heartland: The Reemergence of Geopolitics" 10.

15. Nikolai S. Trubetskoi, "The Upper and Lower Stories of Russian Culture (The Ethnic Basis of Russian Culture)," in Vinkovetsky, ed., *Forebodings and Events*, 82, 83.
16. Ibid., 83.
17. Billington, *Russia in Search of Itself*, 78.
18. Trubetskoi in, *Forebodings and Events*, 83. The Proto-Slavs and Proto-Indo-Iranians formed a group of peoples known as Aryans who inhabited the steppes of southern Russia prior to 1500 B.C. Aryans, called "Axial" peoples by philosopher Karl Jaspers, shared a common culture and spoke a language that later became the origin of several European and Asiatic tongues. Those Aryans who did not migrate westward around 1500 B.C. but remained behind on the Russian steppes, separated into two different peoples who spoke two different forms of Indo-European. One group spoke the Avestan dialect (Proto-Indo-Iranian), the other spoke an early form of Sanskrit (Proto-Slavic-Baltic). It was the Avestan-Aryans who originated Zoroastrianism after Zoroaster, a visionary priest who, around 1200 B.C., claimed that Mazda—one of the three great gods of the Indo-Europeans—was the supreme, universal God who commissioned him to restore order to the steppes plagued by violence. The Avestan Aryans would migrate south across the Caucauses into Persia and India. Those Aryans who were left behind on the Russian steppes would later encounter the Scythians and Sarmatians and the intermingling of these elements, it is believed, would form the immediate ancestors of the Slavs and Balts. See, Karen Armstrong, *The Great Transformation: The Beginning of Our Religious Traditions* (New York: Alfred A. Knopf, 2006), 3-12; also, Mary Boyce, *Zoroastrians: Their Religious Beliefs and Practices*, 2nd ed. (London and New York, 2001); Edwin Bryant, *The Quest for the Origins of Vedic Culture: The Indo-Aryan Debate* (Oxford: University Press, 2001); Colin Renfrew, *Archaeology and Language: The Puzzle of Indo-European Origins* (London, 1987).
19. Armstrong, *The Great Transformation*, 3-12.
20. Ibid.
21. Figes, *Natasha's Dance*, 424.
22. Trubetskoi in, *Forebodings and Events*, 91.
23. Clover, "Dreams of the Eurasian Heartland:" 9. Eurasianism, comments Billington, may turn out to be "the most important train of thought that was hatched among émigrés and brought back to postcommunist Russia." Billington, *Russia in Search of Itself*, 69. Russian proponents of Eurasianism are not alone in revisiting the Mackinder thesis. Zbigniew Brzezinsky, former national security advisor for President Jimmy Carter, and cofounder of the Trilateral Commission, in 1997, authored the book, *The Grand Chessboard: American Primacy and Its Geostrategic Imperatives*, in which he posits that America's "global primacy" resulting from the collapse of the Soviet Union, is dependent on its ability to control the Eurasian continent. "A power that dominates Eurasia," Brzezinsky writes, "would control two of the world's three most advanced and economically productive regions and about three-fourths of the world's known energy reserves." The strategic implications of Brzezinsky's statements were not lost on the second Bush administration. Vice President Dick Cheney's National Energy Policy Report of 2001, published four months before 9/11, recommended placing a priority on "easing U.S. access to Persian [Gulf] supplies." In a report submitted to Cheney by the Council of Foreign Relations in April 2001, American's interest in shaping the destiny of the region is made clear: "American's face long-term energy delivery challenges and volatile energy prices…[I]t is clear that energy disruptions…would affect U.S. national security and foreign policy in dramatic ways…The American people continue to demand plentiful and cheap energy without sacrifice or inconvenience." "Strategic Energy Policy Challenges

for the 21st Century," April 2001, cited in, Anthony Lappe and Stephen Marshall, *True Lies* (New York: Penguin Books, 2004), 50, 51. There can be little doubt that both the Cheney and CFR reports impacted the Bush administration's foreign policy decisions, particularly in its approach to Iraq and Afghanistan.

24. Clover, "Dreams of the Eurasian Heartland:" 10, 11.
25. Billington, *Russia in Search of Itself*, 33.
26. Clover, "Dreams of the Eurasian Heartland:" 12.
27. Ibid., 13.
28. Ibid.
29. Ibid.
30. Ibid., 12, 13.
31. Billington, *Russia in Search of Itself*, 84.
32. Clover, "Dreams of the Eurasian Heartland:" 11. Clover informs us that, outside the State Duma, "Russia's Defense Ministry and military elite have also caught the Eurasian fever." (10) According to Andrew Meier, Eurasianism is "especially strong among the upper ranks of the armed forces and secret services. Even Vympel, the elite *spetsnaz* anti-terrorist squad, has adopted the theory as doctrinal," Meier, *Black Earth*, 340. "The Russian general staff," Dimitri Sims informs us, "is lobbying to add a military dimension to the Shanghai Cooperation Organization, and some top officials are beginning to champion the idea of a foreign policy directed against the West." Additionally, continues Simes: "There are also quite a few countries, such as Iran and Venezuela, urging Russia to work with China with technological assistance in upgrading and modernizing its air force which now includes SU-30 advanced fighter bombers acquired from Russia." (The SU-30 is a version of the SU-27 and its premier fighter, the Chinese-produced fourth generation F-10 aircraft, which is being developed under a cooperation deal between Moscow and Beijing.) Dimitri Simes. "Losing Russia: The Costs of Renewed Confrontation," *Foreign Affairs* (November/December 2007): 51; Jason T. Shapler and James Laney, "Washington's Eastern Sunset: The Decline of U.S. Power in Northeast Asia," *Foreign Affairs* (November/ December 2007): 89.
33. Clover, "Dreams of the Eurasian Heartland:" 11. According to James Billington, Dugin represents the most extreme version of Eurasianism. Billington also labels Dugin as an anti-Semite and regards his view of Eurasianism as having "many of the characteristics of Nazism." Billington, *Russia in Search of Itself*, 81.
34. Clover, "Dreams of the Eurasian Heartland;" 11.
35. Billington, *Russia in Search of Itself*, 81, 82.
36. Clover, "Dreams of the Eurasian Heartland:" 13. See also, Ye. M. Primakov, *The East After the Collapse of the Colonial System* (Moscow: Nauka Publishing House, 1983), Chapter III. After becoming Russia's acting president in 1999, Putin continued Primakov's foreign policy course based on a "multipolar" international order, in response to what he regarded as a hegemonic "unipolar" world built by the United States. With the most recent emergence of differences with the United States over several outstanding issues, Russia's current foreign policy course based on "multipolarism" has concentrated on Asia. In late 2000, Putin abandoned the Gore-Chernomyrdin agreement (1995) whereby Russia consented formally to limit arms sales and nuclear cooperation with Iran. A year later, in July 2001, Putin signed the Russian-Chinese Friendship Treaty, in realization of Primakov's earlier vision of a Moscow-Beijing alliance to counter the United States. See. Mark N. Katz, "Primakov Redux: Putins' Pursuit of 'Multipolarism in Asia," *Demokratizatsiya* 14:1 (Winter 2006): 144-152.
37. Billington, *Russia in Search of Itself*, 77-79. Panarin's viewpoint in reflected in comments Putin made to an unidentified listener at a state dinner in Brussels, Belgium in

2004, in which he sees Europe conjoined with the United States, and Russia 'conceptually linked' with China. Putin's comments are consistent, writes geographer, Arthur Klinghoffer, "with recent Russian strategic analysis which is focused on Russia as a component of the [Eurasian] 'Heartland.'" It sees Eurasia—the "Heartland," "confronted by the 'Atlantic' [i.e., the insular regions], a combination of the U.S. and the western portion of Europe." Eurasia, "is oriented eastward, away from the 'West.' Russia, China, Iran and Iraq, are the key countries...." Russia, in this scheme of things, "is portrayed as a land-based power threatened by sea-based 'Atlanticists,' particularly the U.S. and Britain." To Eurasianists, what is needed is a "security zone" to prevent encroachment by the "Atlanticists"—an alignment of Russia with Eurasian states. In the long run, claim Eurasianists, "[t]he battle is essentially about values, a juxtaposition of Russian uniqueness and the influence of American 'bourgeois liberalism' which signifies moral decline." See, Arthur Jay Klinghoffer, *The Power of Projections: How Maps Reflect global Politics and History* (Westport, CT: Praeger, 2006), 133; also, Robert M. Cutler, "Emerging Triangles: Russia-Kazakhstan-China," *Asia Times*, 4 January 2004. Eurasianism was also the main subject at a closed conference in July 1988 at the Soviet Ministry of Foreign Affairs. See, Milan Hauner, *What is Asia to Us?* (Boston: Unwin Hyman, 1990), 249.

Putin's concerns for Russia's security are not without merit. Parag Khanna, senior research fellow in the American Strategy Program for the neo-conservative New America Foundation, writing in the January 25, 2008 issue of the *New York Times Magazine*, writes that the European Union and the U.S., besides providing a haven for "the likes of Boris Berezovsky to openly campaign against Putin,...also finance and train a pugnacious second-world bloc of Baltic and Balkan nations, whose activists agitate from Belarus to Uzbekistan. Privately," he continues, "some E.U. Officials say that annexing Russia is perfectly doable; it's just a matter of time." Parag Khanna, "Waving Goodbye to Hegemony," *The New York Times Magazine*, 25 January 2008. pp. 37, 39.

38. Clover, "Dreams of the Eurasian Heartland:" 13.

Chapter Five

The New (Moscow) Consensus

World War II left the United States and the Soviet Union as the world's two superpowers. The Cold War marked nearly fifty years of bipolar politics with the two nations and their allies locked in a deadly arms race. When it ended with the dissolution of the Soviet Union in 1991, the United States was left, writes Professor Harm de Blij, "disproportionately powerful in a world where... there would be no clear Number Two."[1]

Russia's sudden resurgence since the turn of the new millennium has released its economic potential and witnessed, due chiefly to the success of Boris Yeltsin's mass privatization program of the 1990s (whose centerpiece was widespread worker ownership), one of the greatest regional transformations in human history. By 2004, the year Yeltsin's successor, Vladimir Putin, was overwhelmingly re-elected as Russia's president, the United States, much to its surprise, found itself confronted , once again, by a powerful, confident Russia ready to compete on nearly equal terms. The "Washington Consensus," America's attempt, through globalization, to imprint its political and economic model on the transitional countries, was now under serious challenge by an emerging new (Moscow) consensus.

The "Washington Consensus," also known as "structural adjustment," was first put forward in 1985 by James Baker, Ronald Reagan's second Secretary of the Treasury. As a solution to mounting Third World default, Baker proposed that, in return for renewed lending by the International Monetary Fund (IMF) and the World Bank, tough new economic reforms, i.e. "structural adjustments", were to be enacted in order to force recipient countries to cut spending on domestic programs such as health care and education, to balance budgets, and to open their economies to Western bank loans to meet their debt obligations. However, contrary to expectations, Baker's "structural adjustment" strategy, in the words of John Kenneth Gailbraith's biographer, Richard Parker, "wrecked further havoc on some of the poorest economies and most vulnerable human beings in the world...." The flood of Western imports which resulted, ravaged small domestic producers who were unable to compete. Adopting monetarist policies did succeed in crushing inflation, Parker admits, but they also retarded growth. Domestic consumption to meet local needs was sacrificed for export-led growth.[2]

In terms of its overall impact on global economic development, the "Washington Consensus" proved disastrous. Writes Parker: "[B]y some estimates, more money was being sent from poor countries than was being spent on the health and education budgets of the entire Third World." The notion (especially favored by neoliberals in the United States) that "markets know best," together with "the coerced 'opening' of dozens of Third World and former Soviet bloc economies in the 1980s and 1990s [including Russia] under the rubric of 'structural adjustment' and 'shock therapy,'" had demonstrated that something was amiss. "[H]alf of the world's population was still needlessly living on less that two dollars per person, and in dozens of countries hundreds of millions of people were suffering more in the 1990s than they had in the 1970s. Most starkly,...more than a million children under the age of five were dying *every month* from preventable malnutrition and disease." Indeed, any major advancement made in reducing global poverty during this period was achieved, not by relying on "the prescriptions advocated by the 'Washington Consensus,'" but, as former Harvard economist, John Kenneth Galbraith revealed, by "strong central government direction of investment and education...."[3]

Globalization's drawbacks have been especially evident in Sub-Saharan Africa, one of the world's poorest regions. There, writes Professor Harm de Blij, "globalization is increasing, not decreasing, the gap between poor and well-off; statistical averages not withstanding," he continues, "the lot of the average African has not improved in the era of globalization....The geographer Robert Stock has described the poverty-stricken condition of the Sub-Saharan cities, many of which are in worse condition today than they were at the end of the colonial era."[4]

In spite of its mostly disastrous consequences, especially for the less developed countries of the Third World few nations have been able to resist what Jim Garrison, president of the State of the World Forum, describes as the "mythic qualities of 'free market' capitalism," which, symbolized by globalization, "represent a veritable 'empire' in its own right..." –with one vital exception. Of all the transitional economies of the post-Soviet era, only Russia (as I pointed out in my earlier book), has demonstrated the determination to elude the "structural adjustments" and "conventionalities" of the all too powerful international financial establishment—the World Bank, the IMF, and the World Trade Organization (WTO)—and its major supporter, the United States—which, "however inadequate, still determine[s] what globalization means, what the rules are, and who is to be rewarded for submission and punished for infractions." The "global empire" which, as self-described "economic hit man" and best-selling author, John Perkins describes, "is rooted in [neoliberal] capitalism" and its mantra the "Washington Consensus" would not, in the eyes of Russia and her leaders, go unchallenged.[5] In challenging the "Washington Consensus," moreover, Russia, if un-intentionally, has set an example for the leaders of the developing nations to emulate as they desperately seek to cope with the grave dislocations caused by globalization. Included among such leaders is Venezuela's mercurial president, Hugo Chavez, whose economic reform program bears a close resemblance to Russian privatization-cum-worker-ownership.

In 2005, Chavez began implementing his "co-management" program which, as worker ownership had in Russia, forms the centerpiece of his economic reforms, by announcing that the Venezuelan government would sell its stake in government-owned enterprises to their workers who would then assume full control of the newly privatized companies.[6] Invepal, a privately-owned paper mill, which had filed for bankruptcy in 2004, was one of the first companies to be affected by the Chavez program. Expropriated by the government, Invepal was then sold to its workers who now control a 49 percent stake and decide on wage and production increases. Worker salaries at Invepal are almost double what they were under the previous management. Alexis Hornebo, who heads Invepal's worker cooperative, says that before the plant became worker-owned, "our opinion never counted."

A pioneer in the co-management program is Pulpus. A start-up diaper company, Pulpus is entirely worker-owned. Workers and shareholders alike must agree on all important decisions, from production levels to personnel decisions. Managers must obtain the worker's consent before an employee is terminated. Differences between the workers and management are resolved with the help of a government mediator who remains in frequent contact with the plant.

Privately-owned companies which choose to participate in the co-management program are promised government loans as an incentive. Under the Chavez plan, companies would share profits with worker cooperatives, as well as give them representation on the boards of directors. In return, the government would provide subsidies in the form of working capital. A portion of the company's profits would be earmarked for social programs in surrounding communities (note the resemblance to social partnerships maintained by Russian worker-owned companies). In order to prevent private owners from attempting to dilute the worker's stake in the company, further government capitalizations would require the approval of 90 percent of board members.

By the end of 2005, approximately 200 mostly small, cash starved private sector companies had voluntarily opted to participate in the co-management program in return for government subsidies. Twenty of these have since gained the approval of the government's co-management team. Four failed companies and two healthy ones were expropriated in 2005 with plans by the government to eventually co-manage all of them. Chavez has vowed that, whenever possible, he will continue to expropriate failed companies and convert them into co-managed firms.

Given the example of Venezuela, one could rightly say that Russia's own determined resistance to American neoliberalism in the form of globalization, has provoked a ripple effect, causing a global chain reaction which has resulted in the emergence of what some are now calling a "new consensus" throughout the world's emerging economies, particularly those in Latin America where the United States has been the dominant power for decades.

Out of the chaos of the early 1990s, Russia's experiment in worker ownership (a core component of binary economics), presented a viable, workable alternative to "the power globalization" to turn "however unevenly, all national economies into a single, global, free [neoliberal] market system. . . conducive to American interests, governed by American norms [and] regulated by American power . . . ."[7] It has also contributed in no small measure to Russia's status as an evolving economic power, a fact highlighted by Russia's presidency of the G-8 in July 2006 at St. Petersburg. At the preliminary G-8 summit meeting of foreign ministers in Moscow in February, Russia put forward several bold proposals, including a debt relief package for the less developed countries (LDCs) by announcing that it will pre-pay $11 to $12 billion of Soviet-era debt to be used to cancel Third World debt.[8] The latter decision was made in response to criticisms from other G-8 members that the Russian economy is too small to be ranked among the eight largest economies in the world and prompted Putin to remark that Russia's presence prevents the G-8 from becoming an "assembly of fat cats." As a transitional economy itself, Russia, he insists, is better able to relate to the economic problems of other emerging economies than are the wealthiest members of the G-8. Russia anticipates becoming a major donor to the International Development Association, the World Bank's lending program for very poor LDCs. Such a move, write reporters Guy Chazan and Michael Phillips, "offer[s] Russia an entry ticket into the elite group of rich donor nations – a huge turnaround for a country that barely eight years age defaulted on its domestic debt and devalued the ruble."[9]

Russia is not alone among the transitional economies in actively opposing globalization. In November 2005, a major setback for the "Washington Consensus" came at a summit of Western hemisphere leaders, when a group of moderate Latin American Leftist leaders, headed by Venezuela's Hugo Chavez, dealt a severe blow to the American-backed proposal for a free-trade zone extending from Alaska to Terra-del-Fuego, Argentina. "Mr. Chavez's success in playing the spoiler role here reflects a harsh fact for the Bush administration," write reporters Matt Moffett and John McKinnon. "Washington can no longer have its way in setting the economic agenda in its own backyard or in a large part of the developing world." Chavez's rise as a major critic of U.S. sponsored trade liberalization, a cornerstone of neoliberalism, "reflects the disappointing results of the ["Washington Consensus"] that [Latin America] and parts of Asia embraced during the 1990s.[10]

Several other Third World leaders, besides Hugo Chavez, have also voiced sharp criticism of the U.S. view of open markets. Correspondent Juan Forero estimates that at least three-quarters of South America is currently under the leadership of center-left presidents who share Chavez's rejection of globalization in their search for a "Third Way" to economic and social progress.[11]

By the end of 2005, despite criticism leveled at the Kremlin throughout 2004 over the so called Khodorkovsky affair (mentioned above), the Russian economy continued to expand for the fifth consecutive year. Industrial production and wages are up and inflation has decreased. By 2006, Russia accumulated a large trade surplus of $120 billion and Central Bank gold and foreign currency reserves (as of April 2006), exceeded $200 billion. Comprehensive tax reform, meanwhile, has placed strong limitations on the number and type of taxes imposed on the various levels of government. Although corruption and capital flight continue to pose serious problems, the ruble has strengthened and is now on the verge of becoming convertible. Russia's GDP reached nearly $1 trillion in 2006, "representing an annual growth of over 25 percent per year, when compared to less than $200 billion in 1999."[12] Powered by high oil and natural gas prices, the value of the ruble rose, in the first half of 2006, 6.7 percent versus the dollar, a trend which analysts expect will continue. Putin, in his annual State of the Nation address on May 10, 2006, announced that by July 1, 2006, the ruble would become fully convertible.[13]

There can be little doubt that these tremendous economic gains of recent years are directly related to Russia's highly favorable, lucrative energy position which comprises approximately 20 percent of her current GDP. In this respect, the Strategic Enterprises, in particular, Gazprom, have played a leading role. As the flagship of the Russian energy sector, Gazprom has become a crucial strategic asset, enabling the Russian government, which controls over 50 percent of the company, to use the "energy card" as a lever in its foreign relations.[14] As the world's largest public energy company by reserves, Gazprom is the model for Russia's other strategic enterprises. As was noted previously, Gazprom provides most of the natural gas to former Soviet republics and to Central Europe, as well as 25 percent of Western Europe's needs. Since 2001, as Michael Freedman and Heidi Brown of *Forbes* inform us, "[Gazprom] has increased earnings from $440 million to $7.5 billion, on $42 billion in sales. It has announced one deal after another and is discussing a pipeline to Japan and a joint venture with Iran. By 2010, it expects to send gas in liquefied state from reserves near the Barents Sea to ports in the U.S. and the company is also looking eastward, with plans to build pipelines to China. In a decade, executives insist, Gazprom's market cap will exceed $1 trillion."[15]

Gazprom's emergence as Russia's "crown jewel," her most important strategic asset, came following Vladimir Putin's assumption to the Russian Federation presidency in 2000, when he began to consolidate the Kremlin's power over Russia's rich store of natural resources, particularly oil and gas. Putin, "seized control of [other] large sectors of the economy [as well], including stakes in autos, aviation, metals, and mining. As chief executive of Russia Inc., he is creating a post-Soviet, post-Yeltsin superpower whose strength comes not from warheads but from commodities."[16] More than any Russian politician before him, Putin has come to realize "the importance of an industry that provides not just heat to the nation's 143 million people but 20 percent of its $77 billion in annual tax revenues." Energy had become "the foundation of Putin's ultimate source of strength" which is based on "the widespread support of the Russian people." Due largely to "the national energy supply, and Putin's ability to exploit it, per capita personal income has increased 29 percent annually since 2001," a fact which, undoubtedly, accounted for much of his high popularity rating.[17]

Putin's willingness to use Strategic Enterprises like Gazprom as an instrument of Russia's foreign relations "was demonstrated in early 2006 by Gazprom's brief suspension of natural gas to Ukraine which, in turn, caused an interruption of supplies to Western Europe. This incident, which exposed the vulnerability of both European and American markets to their dependence on Russian oil and gas, provoked U.S. Vice President Dick Cheney to accuse Russia of using oil and gas as "tools of intimidation or blackmail."[18] Speculation that Gazprom was interested in purchasing a British gas company Centrica, prompted then Prime Minister Tony Blair's government to promise "robust scrutiny" of the deal, only to back down "while Gazprom threatened renegotiate existing long-term gas delivery contract."[19]

The collapse of the Soviet Union which ended the Cold War brought an end to the ideological rivalry between Russia and the United States. In spite of this, however, the two nations failed to become allies with identical perspectives on world events. In discarding the Soviet system, the path that Russia would take toward democracy and capitalism was vastly different from the "Washington Consensus," the course designed by the United States. America, cautions Vladimir Votapek, the former Czech ambassador to Russia, "needs to regard Russia's progress with a different perspective than it applies to itself." The West, he writes, "has to reconcile itself with the unpleasant fact that, after ten years of reform, one-seventh of the world is still very far from the model of democracy and market economics achieved in advanced countries. But does this mean that the West lost Russia? Definitely not. The West has not lost Russia because it never had Russia. The beautiful vision of Russia throwing off its totalitarian ways and integrating among the democratic countries was simply a mistake, and illusion, a fata morgana."[20] Putin, who as president had the support of a large and vocal segment in the State Duma, was in no mood to bring Russia into conformity with the dictates of the "Washington Consensus." By utilizing the "energy card," Putin and his supporters view Russia as a counterweight to the political and economic influence wielded by the United States and European Union. For Russia, using the "energy card," writes analyst Daniel Yergin "is about the state's retaking control of the 'commanding heights' of the energy industry and extending that control downstream, over the critical export pipelines that provide a substantial part of government revenues."[21] No longer content "just to flex its newly developed economic muscle," Russia's new assertiveness is "buoyed [not only] by energy prices," but, "by a desire to define a new role for Russia as an independent power separate and equal to its larger and still wealthiest partners," and, ultimately, "to recover Russia's claim to superpower status, lost in the Soviet collapse."[22]

One area where Russia's increased assertiveness is clearly evident is in the upgrade of its military. After enduring years of benign neglect following the collapse of the Soviet Union, Russia is now modernizing its arsenal of nuclear missiles, forming more than 20 new missile force units, the largest increase since the Cuban Missile Crisis of 1962. In December 2005, a new fleet of ICBMs, comprised of the Topol-M missile with a range of 6,000 miles, went into service. These new missiles are designed to evade anti-ballistic missile systems and possess the capability of changing trajectory in flight. General Nikolai Solovtsov, commander of the Russian missile forces, was quoted as saying that the Topol-M missile, "'is capable of piercing any missile defense system' and is immune to electromagnetic blasts used by current U.S. anti-Ballistic missile systems." A nuclear submarine version of the Topol-M, the Bulava, was successfully tested in September 2005. Colonel General Yuri Baluevsky, the chief of the Russian army's General Staff, earlier in December 2005, cautioned, however, "that nothing aggressive should be read into Russia's action. 'We have long stopped preparing for large-scale nuclear and conventional wars,'" Baluevsky commented to RIA Novosti. "'We will continue to prepare for the defense of our territory, but we will not be preparing for war on foreign land.'"[23]

Currently, Russia spends about 4 percent of its GDP on defense. Since 2003, national defense spending, writes Professor Paul Dibb of the Australian National University, "has doubled in nominal terms (28 percent in real terms.)" Putin had given high priority to the rebuilding of Russia's once mighty military machine. In 2006, defense spending grew by about 20 percent. Increased pay and allowances for military personnel has been matched by rising spending on procurement and R&D. Russia's recent military upgrade also includes "the introduction of innovative 5th generation advanced conventional weapons systems, including missiles, high-speed torpedoes and precision-guided munitions that could challenge U.S. superiority; retention of full-spectrum R&D capabilities that result in military technology breakthroughs; deployment of large formations equipped with modern generations of weapons and technology, along with the retention of the full range of industrial capabilities for equipping high-tech armed forces." Although it is doubtful that the Cold War will return, Professor Dibbs predicts that a "renewed Russia will be strong [and] assertive…[I]t will definitely not be a consistent or reliable partner of the West."[24]

In furthering the goal of reclaiming superpower status, Russia's Strategic Enterprises, as was demonstrated, play a crucial role. The continued dependence of the European Community and the United States on Russia's natural resources, chiefly oil and natural gas, permits the Strategic Enterprise to be utilized to enhance Russia's negotiating position in global affairs, thereby allowing Russia, without sole reliance on her nuclear arsenal, to project its influence far and wide not only in the former Soviet bloc, but throughout the globe.

Notes

1. Harm de Blij, *Why Geography Matters*, 129.
2. Richard Parker, *John Kenneth Gailbraith: His Life, His Politics, His Economics*, 603 – 605. See also, Joseph Stiglitz, *The Roaring Nineties* (New York: W.W. Norton & Co., 2003), 229, 230.
3. Parker, John Kenneth Gailbraith: His Life, His Politics, His Economics, 644- 656.
4. Harm de Blij, *Why Geography Matters*, 267. Also, Robert Stock, *Africa South of the Sahara: A Geographical Interpretation*, 2nd ed. (New York: Guildford Press, 2004).
5. Jim Garrison, *American Empire: Global Leader or Rogue Power?* (San Francisco: Barrett- Koehler Publishers, 2004), cited in John Perkins, *Conscience of an Economic Hit Man* (San Francisco: Barrett-Koehler Publications, 2004), 170. Although Russia has applied for membership in the WTO, as of July 2006, the date of the G-8 summit in St. Petersburg, negotiations were stalled over several unresolved issues. See, James

Hookway, "Waiting for WTO Membership," *Wall Street Journal*, 14 December 2005, A17, A18.

6. Paul Gallegos, "Chavez's Agenda Takes Shape," *Wall Street Journal*, 27 December 2005, A12. Also, Javier Corrales, "Hugo Boss," *Foreign Policy* (January/February 2006): 32-40. Corrales, who takes a dim view of Chavez, describes him as "part provocateur and part electoral wizard."

7. Andrew Bacevich, *American Empire: The Reality and the Consequences of U.S. Diplomacy* (Cambridge, MA: Harvard University Press, 2002), cited in Walden Bello, *Dilemas of Domination: The Unmaking of the American Empire* (New York: Henry Holt & Co., 2005), 28.

8. Andrew E. Kramer, "Finance Ministers Meet Warily in Russia," *New York Times*, 11 February 2006, p. B4.

9. Guy Chazan and Michael Phillips, "Russia Enhances Its G-8 Standing by Paying Debts," *Wall Street Journal*, 8 February 2006, p. A6.

10. Matt Moffett and John D. McKinnon, "Failed Summit Casts Shadow on Global Trade Talks," *Wall Street Journal,* 7 November 2005, pp. A1, A7.

11. Juan Forero, "Letter from South America: Opposition to U.S. markets Makes Chavez a Hero to Many," *New York Times* (International), 1 June 2005.

12. Vladimir Votapek, "Russia's Economic and Political Future: Three Scenarios," cited in Derek C. Mares, ed., *The History of Nations: Russia* (Farmington Hills, Greenhaven Press, 2006), 236, 237.

13. "Notebook" and "Facts and Figures," *Russian Life* (July/August 2006), p. 11.

14. With a value of $305.9 billion, Gazprom is currently the third largest company in the world after Exxon-Mobil and General Electric. In 2005, Gazprom extracted 548 billion cubic meters of gas. "Facts & Figures, *Russian Life* (July/August August 2006), p. 11.

15. Michael Freedman and Heidi Brown, "Energy Tsar," *Forbes*, 24 July 24 2006, p. 95.

16. Ibid., pp. 95, 96.

17. Ibid., pp. 96.

18. Ibid. Some analysts are of the opinion that the Gazprom incident over Ukraine may have been related to pro-Moscow Viktor Yanukovich's political resurgence in Ukraine which resulted from the March 2006 parliamentary elections in which no one party achieved a clear majority. This forced Ukraine's president Viktor Yushchenko, the product of Ukraine's 2004 "Orange Revolution" and a strong supporter of the U.S. and the E.U., to appoint, however reluctantly, Yanukovich, who had been rejected as Ukraine's president in 2004 amidst charges of fraud and corruption, the head of a coalition government. Alan Cullison, "For West, Ukraine Politician's Rebirth Shows Downside of Democracy," *Wall Street Journal*, 4 August 2006, p. A4.

19. Freedman & Brown, "Energy Tsar," 102. Gazprom is not alone in maintaining close ties to the Kremlin. Other Strategic Enterprises include Lukoil, Novatek, natural gas producer that sold 20 percent of its shares to Gazprom, "and so would seem to have the blessing of the government," and Norilsk Nickel which possesses the world's largest nickel reserves. Freedman & Brown, "Energy Tsar," p. 100.

20. Votapek, "Russia's Economic and Political Future, " 204

21. Daniel Yergin, "What Does Energy Security Rally Meal?" *Wall Street Journal*, 11 July 2006, p. A10

22. Steven Lee Mayers and Andrew E. Kramer, "Group of Eight Talks...," New York Times, 13 July 2006, p. A10.

23. "Notebook," *Russian Life* (March/April 2006), p. 8.

24. Paul Dibb, "the Bear is Back," *The American Interest: Policy, Politics and Culture:* II: 2 (November/December 2006): 84, 85. See Also, Steven Rosefielde, *Russia in the 21st Century: The Prodigal Superpower* (Cambridge, UK: The Cambridge University Press, 2005). Rosefielde cautions that Russia has plans to emerge as a full-fledged superpower before 2010.

Chapter Six

New Russia-New Identity

Few historians would disagree that Russia is a country whose norms and standards are essentially different from those of the West. Winston Churchill, Britain's legendary wartime leader, epitomized the popular view of Russia's "otherness" by his famous characterization of Russia as, "a riddle wrapped in a mystery, inside an enigma."[1]

Nowhere is this "otherness" more evident today than in the results of Russia's remarkable transition to a new capitalism and politics. Not only was Russia's political and economic system radically transformed, the country itself was virtually remade, in a word reinvented, in a manner few could have imagined, given over seventy years of one-party rule. Gone is the Communist-led dictatorship, replaced by what historian Thomas Nichols labels, a "presidential democracy" characterized by a multi-party parliament, elections that have largely met international standards for fairness, a relatively free press, and respect for basic civil liberties. With a minimum of violence and bloodshed, the people of Russia and their leaders, in the words of one analyst, "are now engaged in nothing less than designing the basic features of a brand new country."[2]

It is in the economic realm that Russia's "otherness" resulting from the demise of the Soviet system becomes most apparent. In discarding the dysfunctional command system in favor of a market economy, Russia's reformers settled on the unconventional—some would say heretical—theories of Louis Kelso as the starting point for an emerging Russian capitalism. The result was the creation of a new economic paradigm—an alternative to the highly centralized command system of the former Soviet Union and the individualistic, conventional capitalism of the United States. Using binary economics as a guide, Russia's reformers reinvented capitalism by attempting to create an economy that was both efficient and socially just—a "People's Capitalism of broadly shared ownership among most employees and...a market economy that is modified within a firm by a social partnership between government and workers that implies greater economic egalitarianism and greater paternalism, but also higher productivity and quality."[3]

At the center of this new model of economic development is the People's Enterprise based on widespread worker ownership, a core principle of binary economics. "Whatever the intentions of the policy makers," writes Sergey Plekhanov of the Institute for the Study of the U.S. and Canada of the Russian Academy of Sciences, "a new reality...emerged from mass privatization of Russian industry; formally, at least [through worker ownership], managers and workers have equal rights as co-owners of the means of production."

Moreover, the passage by the State Duma in 1998 of Law No. 115 legitimizing worker ownership is evidence that the Russian Federation government is continuing to nurture "the sprouts of a new economy which have become embedded in the Russian soul in the past few years." Indeed, worker ownership in the form of the People's Enterprise, constitutes, states Plekhanov, "a huge potential base for a real democratization of the Russian economy and the introduction of powerful incentives into Russian economic life."[4] In the chaotic process of Russian economic reform, worker ownership through the People's Enterprise, by "appealing to ingrained cultural values, including more of a collectivist ethos among workers and more paternalism among managers," has a clear and significant role to play not only in reforming the economy, but in helping to define Russia's new identity. Reflecting both "the traditional responsibility of enterprises for social welfare, and the lack of such amenities in the public sector," worker-owned enterprises in Russia, will continue, for some time to come, to maintain social partnerships by willingly assuming such heavy responsibilities as providing kindergartens, worker housing, children's camps, and subsidized meals for pensioners.[5]

Alongside the worker-owned People's Enterprise came the appearance of the Strategic Enterprise which, although state dominated, contains a significant degree of worker ownership. These comprise, for the most part, Russia's "blue-chip" companies. Utilizing Russia's immense natural resources—chiefly oil and gas—the Strategic Enterprise has become part of a "national strategic plan" to tighten the Kremlin's control over the country's "natural monopolies" and to further Moscow's interest abroad. As historian Fiona Hill commented to reporter Erin Arvedlund, "[t]he Kremlin wants to set the strategic economic agenda and that means not leaving the long-term strategies and decisions about how revenues should be spent to private companies. The state wants to control the commanding heights." To Vladimir Konovalov of the Petroleum Advisory Forum, a lobbying group for the Russian oil and gas industry: "The Kremlin hopes to create huge, world class operations in important sectors," what he terms, "ship of state" companies which can successfully compete world-wide with other oil and gas giants.[6]

The rising prominence of Strategic Enterprises such as Gazprom and Lukoil has furthered the influence of Russia's energy firms especially in Central and Eastern Europe causing nervousness among recently admitted EU member states that were once part of the Soviet bloc. In neighboring Lithuania, for instance, Lukoil Baltija owns 100 percent of that country's fuel distribution and filling stations. In early 2004, Gazprom bought a 34 percent stake in the national gas distribution company Lietuvos Dujos. Exclaims Janusz Onyszkiewicz, a former Polish Defense Minster who is currently at the Center for International Relations in Warsaw: "We are concerned that Russia backs its oil and gas concerns not as commercial enterprises but as instruments of foreign policy."[7]

Emphasizing the close ties between the Strategic Enterprises of the Russian energy sector and the policies of the Russian Federation government, in January 2002, Putin announced at meetings in Azerbaijan and Turkmenistan a proposal for the establishment of "a Eurasian gas alliance" comprised of Russia, Uzbekistan, Kazakhstan, and Turkmenistan. Led by Russia, the alliance, comment Fiona Hill and Florence Fee, "would coordinate Caspian Basin gas production, ensure Central Asian access to Russian export pipelines, and guarantee long-term Russian purchases of Central Asian gas for its domestic market."[8] By supplying gas to the Russian domestic and export gas system, the proposed gas alliance would not only address concerns over any decline in Gazprom's production, but "ensure Russian energy industry a major role in the construction of any gas pipelines south to Pakistan and India, as well as east to China from Central Asia. Stroitansgas, Russia's pipeline construction company "is emerging as an important player in these projects."[9]

In the oil sector, the state maintains control over several Strategic Enterprises, besides Gazprom, including Rosneft (100 percent), and Slavneft (50 percent with Belarus owning the other half). Additionally, the Russian Federation government has a significant stake in the Eastern Oil Company (37 percent) and in Lukoil (14 percent).[10] While some companies, such as Zarubezneft (considered an arm of the Russian Foreign Ministry) are directed by the state, other companies such as Rosneft and Slavneft, "despite majority state ownership, try to straddle political and commercial imperatives by fighting continuous battles with the government bureaucracy to operate as independently as possible but still access investment capital from state sources." Other private companies, in the meantime, such as Lukoil, "with commercial, market-driven business investment strategies, continue to be strongly influenced by the state."[11]

As Russian Strategic Enterprises extend their operations beyond Russia, not only will they give Russia, predict Hill and Fee, "a significant role to play over the next two decades in helping to diversify world energy supply away from the Middle East," the Strategic Enterprises of the energy sector "will increasingly become the primary means for [Russia] to exert influence abroad." Insider control both by the state together with managers and rank-and-file workers "will leave little room for further foreign penetration of the industry. In the coming decades," they conclude, the Strategic Enterprises of Russia's energy sector, "are likely to become major competitors with the U.S. and other industrial principals... [and] will likely be able to give Shell and Exxon a run for their money in 2020."[12]

Linked to Russia's "otherness" resulting from privatization-cum-worker-ownership is Eurasianism which, like the bold experiment in binary economics, sets Russia off from the West and helps to define her new identity.

Eurasianists, as we have noted previously, view Russian civilization as an amalgam, or blend of many different racial, ethnic, linguistic, and religious elements which date back several thousand years. Russia's "half-way geographical location" located in the center of Halford Mackinder's "world island" between Europe and Asia, writes historian Alexander Chubarov, "has had a profound effect on the emergence of a distinctive civilization, which [is] Asiatic in the eyes of Europeans and too European for the Asians."[13] Both Tsarist and post-Communist Russia "found [their] fitting symbol in the double-headed eagle of

Byzantium, with one of its crowned heads turned to the east and the other, to the west," epitomizing "the dual nature of a great state that extends for thousands of miles across two continents." Comprised of an "extraordinary diverse mix of peoples," Russia, Chubarov reminds us, has always been "vulnerable to the danger of being torn apart by the incompatibility of the cultures it had brought together into one empire over the course of many centuries."[14]

Russia's unique 'half-way" geography resulted in the formation of an empire "whose growth took a direction unfamiliar to western Europeans." Write professors Karen Darvish and Bruce Parrott: "Thanks to the vast openness of the Eurasian steppe, Tsarist Russia, in contrast to the pattern later exhibited by Western European imperialism, colonized territories that were contiguous rather than physically separate from the metropole."[15] As a consequence, Russians and non-Russians mingled "more extensively than they would have if the colonies had been situated on another continent." The creation of the modern Russian nation, therefore, "did not precede the process of tsarist colonial expansion, but instead coincided with it." Occurring simultaneously, "the two processes blurred the ethnic and cultural definition of Russian nationality...." In contrast to the English and French who "had no doubt where they stood in relation to their colonies for they never identified them with the homeland," Russians "have always lived among non-Russians" and have for centuries viewed Russia as a multi-national state.[16]

A modern variant of the historic struggle that in the nineteenth and early twentieth-centuries divided Westernizers from Slavophiles is the foreign policy debate in post-Soviet Russia between advocates of an "Atlanticist" or a "Eurasian" orientation for Russia.[17] From the perspective of the Atlanticists "the West is no longer an adversary of Russia, but a model for Russian emulation and a partner in post-Soviet world order." In the economic sphere, Atlanticists can be grouped alongside those reformers who, like Yegor Gaidar, Anatoli Chubais and their American sponsors, favored the neoliberal approach to economic reform based on "shock therapy," a rapid transition to a market economy. By contrast, "the exponents of a Eurasian outlook believe that Russia should concentrate on expanding its ties with the nations of the Middle East and Asia where," according to Darvish and Parrott, "it can command greater influence [because of its large Turkic-Muslim population] and can fulfill its historic calling as an international leader and great power."[18] Because Eurasianism, like Russia's experiment in binary economics (which created a reformed economy dominated by the worker-owned enterprise), also stresses Russia's uniqueness arguing that Russia need not, indeed should not, Westernize (read Americanize) to achieve modernity, advocates of a Eurasian outlook can be generally grouped with those reformers favoring a gradualist approach to economic reform based on worker ownership, a central tenet of binary economics.

In the process of redefining itself in the twenty-first century, Russia, Dawisha and Parrott concur, "will be compelled to struggle with a recurring issue of [its] history: the relationship of Russia to the West."[19] Whether, in the coming decades of the new century Russia will pursue a path similar or fundamentally different from the West in defining its new identity, will depend on the resilience of her political and economic reforms to survive the many changes that lay ahead. Unique among these reforms in their overall impact is Russia's bold experiment in binary economics which was so successful in transforming the post-Soviet system. Adapted to special conditions in Russia, binary economics, the central feature of which was widespread worker ownership, by broadening capital ownership to include millions of ordinary Russians, reinvented capitalism by attempting to create an economy that was both efficient and socially just—a People's Capitalism which, together with Eurasianism with its emphasis on Russia's age-old traditional connections with the "Turanian East," form the underpinnings not only of a new national identity but of a "Moscow Consensus"—a "Third Wave" between communism and conventional capitalism and, as such, pose a direct challenge to the neoliberal policies of the "Washington Consensus."

Notes

1. Alexander Chubarov, *The Fragile Empire: A History of Imperial Russia* (New York: Continuum, 1999), 4. "Part of the task of students in the West studying Russian intellectual history," writes Lesley Chamberlain, "was to show that the mystery was susceptible to Western understanding; and in that respect to show that Russia could be brought into line with an enlightened postwar world. It seems to me clear that Russia was never necessarily any of these things. It remained a 'motherland,' intelligible to itself perhaps, but poorly grasped from outside...Russia and the West are neither compatible nor incompatible just enduringly 'other' and faintly uncomfortable in each other's company. For as long as this was not admitted, it was a kind of invented geocultural snobbery for historians to say, in effect, ah, this wild, sad country, we can find a place for it yet, in our wisdom. The Russian, even in moods of deep self-criticism, do not see themselves like this. The world is simply their own." Lesley Chamberlain, *Motherland*, xii.

2. Thomas Nichols, *The Russian Presidency, Society and Politics in the Second Russian Republic* (New York: Palgrave, 1999). Also, Jude Wanninski, "The Future of Russian Capitalism," *Foreign Affairs* (Spring 1992), cited in Matthew A. Kaljic, ed., *The Breakup of Communism* (New York: The H.W. Wilson Co., 1993), 102. Much has been mentioned of late about Russia's recent "retreat" from democracy. The pull-out of OSCE observers from Russia in the days leading up to the December 2007 parliamentary elections, has prompted charges of poll-rigging, among other things, which as reporter Neil Buckley writes, "[e]ven the [Kremlin's] staunchest critics do not believe...is needed to ensure victory for the pro-Putin party," although "there may be a temptation to boost its majority and turn out high figures." Because of Putin's "sky high popularity," Buckley notes, he "could almost certainly win free elections subjected to full scrutiny." In point of fact, "[m]uch of what is happening now [in Russia] seems a response to Ukraine and Georgia's colored revolutions. The Kremlin sees these as coups engineered by an unholy alliance of Western observers, diplomats, security services, non-governmental bodies, and exiled Russian 'oligarchs' eager to do the same in Russia." Neil Buckley, "The Paradox of Russia's Retreat from Democracy," *Financial Times*, 17/18 November 2007, p. 9.

3. Logue, Plekhanov and Simmons, *Transforming Russian Enterprises*, 262.

4. Plekhanov, "The Road to Employee Ownership in Russia," in Logue, Plekhanov and Simmons, *Transforming Russian Enterprises*, 69.

5. Logue, Plekhanov and Simmons, *Transforming Russian Enterprises*, 266, 267. This demonstration of social responsibility on the part of worker-owned enterprises toward the well-being of their workers and the community, we are reminded by political scientist Vladimir Martynov, is deeply rooted in the age-old Russian tradition of the *kollektiv* (the collective Russian soul). See, Eric Helque, "Boom Time: Siberia's Oil-Rich Middle Class," *Russian Life* (May-June 2004), 59, 62. The primary socioeconomic unit of Russia's traditional social organization, we are told, "was a corporate-collectivist formation based not on the principle of private ownership, as in the West, but on collective or state ownership (e.g., village commune, association of artisans, collective and state farms, cooperatives, etc.). In terms of social partnerships, the operation of the People's Enterprise embodies most of these same principles. Chubarov, *The Fragile Empire*, 13, 14.

6. Erin E. Arvedlund and Simon Romero, "Kremlin Reasserts Hold on Russia's Oil and Gas," *New York Times*, 17 December 2004, pp. A1, C2.

7. "Ivan at the Pipe" (Special Report: Russian Energy Firms), *The Economist*, 11 December 2004, pp. 67-69. Also, John Rossant, David Fairlamb and Jason Bush, "Continental Divides: As EU Expansion Nears, Relations with Russia are Getting Tense," *Business Week*, 22 March 2004, 72, 73.

8. Fiona Hill and Florence Fee, "Fueling the Future: The Prospects for Russian Oil and Gas," *Demokratizatsiya*, 10:4 (Fall 2002): 475.

9. Ibid.

10. Ibid., see also, U.S. International Energy Agency, "Russian Energy Survey 2002," March 2002, 66-70.

11. Ibid.: 475, 476.

12. Ibid.: 483.

13. Chubarov, *The Fragile Empire*, 7.

14. Ibid.

15. Karen Dawisha and Bruce Parrott, *Russia and the New States of Eurasia: The Politics of Upheaval* (Cambridge, UK: University Press, 1994), 26.

16. Chubarov, *The Fragile Empire*, 7. Over the centuries, Russia's political identity was heavily dependent on its imperial exploits and the national state was made identical with the empire. In the twentieth-century, Russia's identity, we are told, "continued to hinge on the international power of the state—but [after 1917] on the power of the Soviet state whose millenarian ideology contained a strong imperial element." Following the collapse of the Soviet Union, however, Russia became the only world power in recent memory to peacefully relinquish all of its once mighty empire without being defeated by war. Russia has also voluntarily given up superpower status and is making the attempt in the post-Soviet era to reevaluate her greatness as a nation closer to home territory. Dawisha and Parrott, *Russia and the New States of Eurasia*, 30, 31. Also, Dimitry Simes, "America and the Post-Soviet Republics," *Foreign Affairs*, 7:3 (Summer 1992): 86.

17. Dawisha and Parrott, *Russia and the New States of Eurasia*, 30, 31.

18. Ibid., 31. See also, A. Rahr, "'Atlanticists' versus 'Eurasianists' in Russian Foreign Policy," RFE/RL Research Report, 1; 22 (1992): 17-22.

19. Ibid.

Conclusion

It's All About Economics

In 1988, Yale University professor, Paul Kennedy, in his best-selling book, *The Rise and Fall of Great Powers*, argued that a nation's economic and industrial strength, in great measure, determines its military power and its global status. He also made the claim that U.S. power, relative particularly to China, Japan, and the European Union, was on the decline, and in its foreign policy, he accused the U.S. of "imperial overstretch."[1] Although Professor Kennedy's predictions about the U.S. proved premature, his original thesis about the importance of a nation's economy relative to its global power position is still quite valid.

Almost a decade later, came Samuel Harrington's 1996 book, *Clash of Civilizations*.[2] Huntington reconfigures world politics along "cultural fronts," dividing the world into 11 geographic realms with Russia as one of the eleven. Conflicts in the twenty-first century, he predicts, will take the form of civilizational clashes which "will erupt as cultural "fault line wars."' Remaking the world order in the new millennium "will essentially pit the 'West Against the Rest.'" No longer present will be the "intensive geographic consensus of the 1960s" which was predicated by the great superpower rivalry between the U.S. and the Soviet Union. This will yield to "culturally discrete entities whose internal cohesion is in large part based on growing antipathy to the West."[3] With the end of the Cold War, the West of the 1960s "has become quadripolar [North, Central, and South America, plus Europe] with an assertive superpower United States in an increasingly contentious relationship with a wary Europe and contentious ties to unpredictable Russia even as Brazil and greater South America loom larger on the strategic stage."[4]

All things considered, "in the context of the mesh of civilizations, it is clear," writes Professor de Blij of Michigan State University, "that any transformation of the world order during the twenty-first century will still be primarily the function of states not 'civilizations.'" Among the "putative contestants," alongside what de Blij predicts will be the U.S., China and India, will most assuredly also include the Russian Federation which, curiously, despite Russia's enormous size and wealth both in human and natural resources (especially oil and gas), most analysts of the world scene today, including Professor de Blij, exclude.[5] Contrary to what most analysts predict, the long term challenge to Western, especially U.S. supremacy, will come not so much from China or India as from Russia. A major factor which will tip the geopolitical scale in Russia's favor is energy, "Russia's silver lining." Currently (as of 2008), Russia holds the lion's share of the world's energy resources (2nd in oil production; first in natural gas). Using these as leverage, Russia will be able to exert enormous pressure in its foreign policy pursuits.

In view of Russia's continuing economic growth averaging around 5 percent per annum—caused, in large measure, by the success of her economic reforms whose centerpiece, as we have noted, was widespread worker ownership, a cardinal principle of binary economics—it is possible to predict, as several influential Russia-watchers have done, that in the very near future, a Russian economic miracle, *economicheskoe chudo*, might very well occur not unlike that of Japan in the 1960s, or, more recently, Ireland in the 1990s.

One such observer is Liam Halligan, an economic expert with the Russian-European Policy Institute in Moscow who, in offering his thoughts on what the future holds for Russia's economy following Boris Yeltsin's dramatic come-from-behind reelection victory in July 1996, commented that Yeltsin's defeat of Gennady Zyuganov, the Russian Communist Party leader "paved the way for a decade of economic growth that will silence the skeptics and even surprise the optimists."[6]

Another keen observer of the current economic scene in Russia with an upbeat view of the Russian economy is financial guru, J. Mark Mobius, head of the Templeton Emerging Markets Group. When asked by the influential bi-weekly, *Russia Review*, to comment on what the future holds in store for Russia's economy, Mobius declared that Russia is "a country about ready to take off," surpassing not only Japan but possibly the United States as well. "It is very, very exciting because I see the same characteristics I saw in Japan. You see the same awakening, the same impact of something new coming into a culture and changing the way people think."[7] Mobius goes even further by predicting that Russia, in GDP terms, could overtake the U.S. "There are many sectors where they could [do this], such as oil and gas, power, natural resources, heavy machinery, heavy industry. They've got all the ingredients. They've got manpower. They've got the educated workforce. We are looking at a country that is going to go places."[8] True, these optimistic comments were made two years prior to the 1998 financial collapse. Be that as it may, Russia's recent economic recovery—especially evident since the turn of the new millennium—vindicates Mobius's earlier remarks.

In forecasting a promising economic future for Russia, Mobius is joined by Professors Daniel Yergin and Thane Gustavson who, in their 1993 book (updated and revised in 1995), *Russia 2010 and What It Means for the World*, put forward several possible scenarios, or "histories" of Russia's future, one of which includes, *chudo*, the Russian word for "miracle" which, in their words, "has the connotation of something out of wonderland. Skeptics around the world waste no time in dismissing it as a fable, a dream. Yet the slogan appeals to the new Russian businessmen," among the chief beneficiaries of privatization-cum-worker ownership. "It also captures the imagination of many Russian young adults. Would it be possible to have an economic miracle in Russia? Why not?" Yergin and Gustafson confidently conclude.[9] In point of fact, Russia's economic prospects, write Yergin and Joseph Stanislaw, "could turn out to be better than is conventionally expected. Despite the differences, the analogy of Japan's economic miracle is relevant." Russia possesses a highly educated workforce with considerable skills. "For the first time in seven decades, its great scientific and technical capabilities are linked to the marketplace—something heretofore impossible." A post-Soviet generation of youthful men and women has already emerged, eager to partake in the building of a modern economy. "An enormous pent-up demand for goods and services, built up over seven decades," is now being satisfied as consumer spending explodes. Russia, now open to global trade and commerce, "is tied to the world community by the enabling technologies of computers, the Internet, telephone, and fax. Indeed," exclaim Yergin and Stanislaw, "the impact of being plugged into the world economy after three-quarters of a century of isolation could prove enormous."[10]

Highlighting the possibility of a Russian economic miracle in the near future is the fact that Russia is already an industrial powerhouse, albeit "a misshapen one," according to some, with an economy which at the beginning of the 1990s—prior to the collapse of the Soviet Union—was seven times larger than the rapidly expanding economy of China, one of today's fastest growing economies.[11] In spite of its many shortcomings, Russia today possesses several distinct advantages from which a *chudo* could emerge.[12] To begin with, besides being a vast storehouse of oil and natural gas, Russia has a surplus capacity of many raw and semi-processed materials, such as fertilizer and metals. She also possesses abundant and relatively low-wage scientific and engineering personnel, as well as a trained and literate work force. There is an excess capacity in many industrial plants, pipelines and railroads, some of which contain capital stock that is new and relatively efficient. Throughout the country, there is a wealth of unexploited managerial talent and energy. Add to these factors the enormous (abovementioned) pent-up demand for consumer goods and services, plus a growing middle class and a rising standard of living, and one has most of the major ingredients for rapid if not spectacular economic growth.[13]

A key indicator of a country's economic growth potential is gross domestic product and per capita income. In 1996, Russia was ranked eighth—seventh without China—at over $900 billion in GDP. As was noted, since 2000, Russia's economic growth rate annually has averaged 7 percent. In the next five to ten years, even with a moderate growth rate, Russia is expected to increase its GDP to well over $1 trillion, which, if achieved, would rank her among the world's richest nations alongside the United States, Canada, Japan, Germany, France, the United Kingdom, and Italy. In June 1997, Russia attended, for the first time, the G-7 meeting held in Denver, Colorado—dubbed the "Summit of Eight,"—and was subsequently admitted into the prestigious Group of Seven nations. In July 2006, Russia, played host to the G-8 which was held in President Putin's hometown of St. Petersburg.

In terms of per capita income, Russia, in 1997, ($5,190), was placed by Dun & Broadstreet, far ahead of other former Communist countries, including Poland ($2,500), and the Czech Republic ($3,155), both regarded as two of the more successful transitional economies. Russia at that time was also well ahead of

South Africa ($3,000), Brazil ($3,452), Chile ($3,627), Thailand ($2,423), and Turkey ($2,192), countries which are today among the fastest growing emerging economies. Over the last five years, as was previously noted, since the turn of the new millennium, dollar per capita income in Russia has risen by nearly 29 percent per annum, faster even than China.[14] In terms of future growth potential, Barbara Peitsch, an analyst at Santander Investment, places Russia on the same level as Hungary, Poland, and Kazakhstan. Particularly impressive to Peitsch is the Russian savings rate which, in 1996, was close to 27 percent of GDP. As of 2006, 70 percent of all income in Russia is disposable, compared to 40 percent for the average Western consumer.[15]

One of the main reasons why so many Russians appear prosperous, despite the fact that they earn, on average, only a few hundred dollars per month ($300), has to do with prices, particularly for non-traded goods, such as housing, public transport, heating and electricity, the costs of which, in spite of continuing inflation, are still remarkably low in comparison to the West. This is due, in part, to several factors—low labor costs, government subsidies, and price controls. In view of these factors, a Russian on a net salary of $500 per month may have as much disposable income as a Western European earning three times as much. The average Russian consumer may own, free of debt, a *dacha* or an apartment that in the West could cost more than $1,000 per month in rent or in mortgage payments. Building a *dacha* in the country (the Russian equivalent of the "detached" or "single-family" home), was not only a way of saving in the Soviet era, but supplied many Russian families with most of their fresh fruit and vegetables for the cold winters months, thus cutting down on the cost of food. In addition, in Russian cities, public transport is readily available, highly subsidized and cheap to afford. As in Soviet times, child care remains relatively inexpensive since much of it is still provided free by the enterprise where one is employed, making it financially feasible for Russian mothers to work outside the home to supplement the family income. Clothing also costs considerably less than in the West.[16]

Contributing in no small measure to Russia's recent economic recovery is the small business sector which is being sparked by increased consumer confidence and an upsurge in spending. According to GosKomstat and the State Committee for the Support and Development of Small Business, between 1992 and 1997, small businesses comprised 12 percent of Russia's GDP. By the turn of the century, this figure was projected to increase to between 15 and 17 percent of the GDP. Paul Ansel of the U.S.-Russia Investment Fund, writes that "small business is particularly important in transition economies such as Russia where emerging growth companies must compensate for the decline in the industrial sector. The Russian government," he continues, "estimates that small business added more than 1 million jobs and [in 1997] employ[ed] more than 14 million people in 810,000 companies." Small business, which most analysts agree is the bedrock of a truly successful market economy, writes Ansel, "was expected to triple by the year 2000."[17]

As of November 2005, despite persistent criticism leveled at the Kremlin throughout 2004 over the Khodorkovsky affair, the Russian economy continued to expand and to attract outside investment. "Inflows of foreign direct investment rose in the first half of [2005]" writes reporter Guy Chagin, "by 30 percent from a year earlier to $4.5 billion. Russia's RTS stock index had risen by 55 percent since mid-May. Russia's credit rating was upgraded by Fitch Ratings and by Moody's Investment Service in October." There has also been a marked slowdown in the capital flowing out of Russia.[18]

Awash in petrodollars, plans are underway to complete long delayed Soviet-era projects such as the unfinished Boguchansk hydroelectric dam in Siberia and the half-completed Baikal-Amur railway. The Kremlin has also promised to raise doctor's salaries, and to increase social spending. Following his appointment to first deputy Prime Minister, Dimitry Medvedev, the recently elected President of the Russian Federation, announced to Russian reporters, that he intends to utilize some of the wealth derived from Russia's economic resurgence to focus on social programs, "to help raise the living standard of every living Russian," reflecting outgoing President Putin's determination to improve government services and to raise living standards.[19]

In making the transition from a command economy to a market system, Russia today finds itself astride two competing economic worlds. On the one hand, to use Mackinder's term, is the "insular world" represented principally by the United States, and tied together by NAFTA, NATO, the EU, and the international financial system—the World Bank and the IMF. We may label this world, the Trilateral component, made up primarily of the G-7 nations. Symbolic of the "insular world's" economic philosophy is what Joseph Stiglitz and others have termed the "Washington Consensus"—a modern American-style version of capitalism which, in the immediate aftermath of the Soviet Union's downfall in 1991, became "the basic strategy for development (and for managing crises and the transition from communism to the market) advocated, beginning in the 1980s, by the IMF, the World Bank, and the U.S. Treasury...." Also referred to as "neoliberalism," the "Washington Consensus," involved "minimizing the role of government through privatizing state-owned enterprises and eliminating government regulations and interventions in the economy. Government had a responsibility for macrostability, [which] meant getting the inflation rate down [but] not getting the unemployment rate down."[20]

To its critics, neoliberal capitalism symbolized by the "Washington Consensus," also includes "increasing concentrations of ownership [corporate concentration], and disparities of income, the high (and heartless) efficiency of the capitalist market economy and—presumably—a Western style intervention welfare state to ameliorate the consequences of what otherwise would be poverty and cyclical collapse."[21] This was the paradigm utilized by Yegor Gaidar and Anatoly Chubais in the immediate aftermath of the Soviet Union's demise, to virtually demolish the command system in one fell swoop. This radical "fast-track" approach to economic reform in Russia came to be identified as "shock therapy," and was a dismal failure resulting in Gaidar's replacement as Yeltsin's deputy prime minister.

The other competing economic world is the "world island" whose so called "heartland" is Russia, which, because of its size and location, is the most powerful country in terms of its combined military, political and economic prowess. Close behind Russia are China, India and the members of the Shanghai Cooperative Organization—the "Shanghai Five" (SCO), which, besides Russia, China, and the former Soviet Central Asian republics, Kazakhstan and Uzbekistan, includes Mongolia, Pakistan, India and Iran as associated members. We might label this world region the Eurasian component made up chiefly of the "Big Three," Russia, China and India. Together these countries make up over 2.2 billion of the world's population. Indeed, the GDP of the "Big Three" exceeds that of the G-7 nations combined.

Symbolic of the "world island" in terms of economics is Russia's development toward a "'popular capitalism' [People's Capitalism] of broadly shared ownership among most employees [a fundamental tenet of binary economics] and a market economy...modified...by a social partnership between management and workers...." People's Capitalism "also implies far more of a welfare function for the firm than is typical in the United States or Western Europe." Popular or People's Capitalism, moreover, calls for a gradual as opposed to a rapid or "fast-track" transition to a market economy.[22] In People's Capitalism, ownership not salary alone is regarded as the true path to real wealth and prosperity. Worker ownership (the essence of People's Capitalism and binary economics), by making the worker an actual stakeholder in the company in which he is employed, binds the worker to the company more surely than does a high wage alone. The manipulation of the work force only to provide maximum profits is no longer defensible under worker ownership as it is under the "rationalistic capitalistic organization of labor" of conventional, neoliberal capitalism. In a word, under worker ownership, capitalism is reinvented.

It is my studied opinion that Russia's new identity—her "otherness"—in the twenty-first century, will be defined not as much by language, religion, politics or culture, as by her evolving economic system centered on broad-based capital ownership, a core principle of binary economics, first proposed by San Francisco attorney Louis Kelso in the late 1950s, adopted by Soviet economic reformers in the late 1980s, and made the centerpiece of Boris Yeltsin's mass privatization program of the early 1990s.

All of which brings us back to Paul Kennedy's abovementioned thesis about the importance of economics to a nation's overall strength and future prospects. Marx postulated that economics is the driving force of history and politics. And so it is in the twenty-first century. The ability of nations to project their power and influence will rely primarily on economics, that is to say, on the strength of their economies to successfully compete in the global market place. Situated in the "heartland" of Mackinder's "world island," astride Europe and Asia, Russia, due to its enormous size and location geographically, possesses a tremendous comparative advantage. This is especially evident in the areas of land and seaborne transportation. In respect to the former, the 6,000 mile-long Trans-Siberian railroad (Trans-Sib), carries most of the container traffic between East Asia and Europe, forming a transcontinental land bridge through the vast Central Asian corridor connecting St. Petersburg on the Baltic to Vladivostok on Russia's Pacific coast. The shorter distance and travel time between the Far East and Western Europe utilizing the Trans-sib will mean that transcontinental land routes could eventually replace the longer, more time consuming oceanic routes as the main avenue of global commerce by the mid-twenty-first century.[23] Running parallel to the Trans-Sib is the transcontinental highway whose final phase, now under construction, is scheduled for completion by 2010.[24]

Global warming, meanwhile, will make the now perennially ice-bound Arctic Ocean more accessible to year-round navigation along the Northern Sea Route (NSR), a waterway developed by the Soviets to provide a connection with the Far East. In spite of the use of powerful icebreakers, which include nine nuclear-powered vessels, navigation along the entire length of the NSR from its western terminus at Murmansk to the Bering Sea, is possible, currently, for only four months of the year. Today, the NSR is open to international shipping and with global warming accompanied by the further melting of the Arctic ice sheet, the NSR is certain to become a very attractive route.[25] The distance between Hong Kong and the European ports north of London is shorter via the NSR than through the Suez Canal. Moreover, Russia is very anxious to develop the NSR as an alternative to exporting goods by way of Ukraine, Belarus, and the Baltic states. The seaborne traffic in oil and liquefied natural gas emanating from locations along Russia's far northern coast will mean that pipelines will no longer be the sole outlets for their export to world markets.

The above developments, it should be noted, could lead to Russia eventually controlling much if not most of the transcontinental carrying-trade between Europe and Asia by mid-century or sooner. International commerce utilizing the Trans-Sib in natural resources (timber and minerals) and freight, together with ocean-going trade from the Arctic in oil and liquefied natural gas, by 2020, could very well exceed or come close to exceeding world oceanic traffic across both the Atlantic and Pacific both in volume as well as value of product. This, along with Russia's huge manufacturing base, its highly skilled and educated work force and favorable balance of trade with the West (the U.S. and E.U.), will enable it to mount a serious challenge to the United States and to the West with the actual prospect of someday altering the world balance of power in Russia's favor. In such a situation, the U.S. and its European partners will have few options but to accept, however reluctantly, Russia's enhanced status as a dominant global player. Russia's new energy status, moreover, could conceivably reduce America and its NATO allies to the role of junior partners in developments which will be controlled by the Kremlin.

Russia's energy status may also involve its insistence in exercising authority over the foreign and security policy of adjacent countries, especially Belarus, the Baltic states of Estonia, Latvia and Lithuania, and Ukraine. Given the political situation at the time, there may even emerge a Slavic political and economic troika consisting of Russia, Belarus and Ukraine (the "Slavic Coreland") dominated by Russia. It is conceivable that, in the not too distant future, a reintegration of the Slavic nations could take place around Russia. In the case of Belarus, this may have already occurred. In 1994, the monetary systems of Belarus and Russia were unified. In exchange for preferential access to Russian oil, natural gas and other resources, Belarus relinquished sovereignty over its currency and banking system. A year later, in a 1995 referendum, an overwhelming majority of Belorussians voted in favor of closer economic integration with Russia and to recognize Russian as the official language of Belarus. In early 1996, a "union state" was formed between Russia and Belarus whose purpose was to closely integrate the economies, political system, and cultures of the two countries.[26]

Not everyone is at ease with what has become labeled by its critics as "reintegration." Dimitry Trenin, deputy director of the Carnegie Moscow Center for International Peace, and a staunch advocate of Russia's close integration with the West, steadfastly opposes reintegration which he labels "revisionism" and which he equates with Eurasianism. "In simple policy terms," he writes, "[revisionism] means the restoration of Russian domination over the entire Soviet/imperial space and the adjacent territorial spheres of influence. The union with Belarus," he continues, "is thus viewed as only the first step, to be followed by a 'trilateral union' with [now defunct] Yugoslavia, an eventual 'second reunification' with Ukraine, and a new 'voluntary' association by Armenia, Kazakhstan, Kyrgyzstan and potentially other post-Soviet states." The revisionist (Eurasianist) model, he goes on to say, "implies competition and conflict with the West in the former Soviet space, the Balkans, and Central Europe." To oppose "the immense capabilities and resources of the West, revisionists propose creating a new Eastern bloc made up of Russia and the CIS [Commonwealth of Independent States], China, India, and Iran." Such a "Eurasian dream," should it ever be realized, would confront America, Trenin warns, "with what it fears most: the nightmare of a Eurasia united in a single power structure"—i.e., the domination of Mackinder's "heartland" by a powerful alliance of Eurasian nations with Russia in the lead, whose primary task, according to leading Eurasianist advocate Alexandr Dugin, "would be to wrestle away the rimlands from U.S. domination and turn them into anti-American allies." In an endnote, Trenin reminds us that "[t]hese motifs are recurrent in the speeches of Zyuganov, Zhirinovsky and Sergei Baburin," all staunch supporters of Eurasianism.[27] Indeed, there are many Russian democrats, James Billington writes, who "express sympathy for some eventual peaceful modification of Russia's borders. Most Russians," he continues, "favor unification with Belarus. Many share Solzhenitsyn's hope that reintegration might someday also be worked out with Ukraine. Like Solzhenitsyn, the liberal scholar Igor Zevwlev adds to the list Northern Kazakhstan, which, like parts of Ukraine, is heavily populated with ethnic Russians."[28]

Whatever the outcome, one can be certain that, for the foreseeable future, as a major military, political and economic power in control of one-seventh of the earth's surface with an enormous storehouse of natural resources and human talent, Russia will remain a significant world force and continue to exert a major role in the process of global transformation.[29]

Notes

1. Paul Kennedy, *The Rise and Fall of Great Powers* (New York: Random House, 1987).
2. Samuel P. Huntington, *The Clash of Civilizations and the Remaking of the World Order* (New York: Simon & Schuster, 1996).
3. deBlij, *Why Geography Matters*, 122, 123.
4. Ibid., 122.
5. In his "world boundary framework" of "four megastates that are approximately coincident with 'civilizations,'" Professor deBlij cautiously includes "Orthodox-Christian Russia" but with the disclaimer, "whose cultural and demographic decline render it an unlikely participant in the process of global transformation except as a flank to the West." Ibid., 124.
6. Liam Halligan, "How Russia Will Thrive," *Russia Review*, 9 September 1996, p. 8. Sadly, the financial collapse of August 1998 would seriously dampen much of this earlier enthusiasm.
7. Mark Mobius, "We May Be Looking at a Country that is Really Going to Go Places," *Russia Review*, 26 August 1996, p. 12.
8. Ibid. One of these sectors, as Jason Bush of *Business Week* points out is in steel production. "Russian steel makers," he writes, "are in the midst of an assault on the U.S. market," investing more than 3 billion in U.S. operations in the past three years." Severstal, Russia's number two producer, which purchased Rouge Industries Inc., in Detroit (see above, chapter 4), is also an 80 percent shareholder in SeverCorr, an $800 million mill currently being constructed in Columbus, Mississippi, which, when completed, will nearly double Severstal's American production to 5.8 million tons yearly, "making the company one of the top five integrated steel producers in the U.S." Over the next four years, we are told, Severstal North America Inc., plans an additional $1 billion in investments. Meanwhile, the SeverCorr facility "will be the first to use an electric furnace for automotive steel, a less labor-intensive—and more cost-effective—technology." SeverCorr's likely customers include Toyota plants in Kentucky and Texas "and the operations of other European and Japanese automakers now moving into the American South." Severstal's confidence in its U.S. operations is reflected by another Russian steel producer Evraz which, in 2006, purchased Oregon Steel in Portland for $2.3 billion. One focus at Evraz's Oregon plant has been to increase the competitiveness of its U.S. operations by utilizing its low-cost production operations in Russia. This is being done by shipping to the U.S., "slab" steel which is then further processed in the U.S. to manufacture final products such as heavy plate used in construction. Evraz is also seeking to replicate the technical knowledge of its U.S. operations about specialist steels which are used in high-speed rail and in leak-proof large diameter pipes required to transport gas and oil to the company's Russian plants in order for them to be able to produce higher-value types of steel. See, Jason Bush, "Russia's Steel Wheels Roll Into America," *Business Week*, 1 October 2007, p. 44; articles by Peter Marsh, "Severstal Plans $1 Billion Investment in the U.S.;" "Détente Between Steelmakers Part of a Russian Industrial Revolution," *Financial Times*, 31 December 2007, p. 16.

9. Yergin and Gustafson, *Russia 2010*, 160. Like Yergin and Gustafson, Richard Layard and John Parker, co-authors of *The Coming Russian Boom*, also predict a Russian economic miracle. With Russia currently experiencing strong economic growth, Layard and Parker forecast that, by 2010, Russia will become the economic wonder of the world, outstripping Poland, Hungary, and even China.

10. Daniel Yergin and Joseph Stanislaw, *The Commanding Heights: The Battle Between Government and the Marketplace that is Remaking the Modern World* (New York: Simon & Schuster, 1998), 293. Professor Paul Dibb of the Australian National University cites four major reasons for Russia's resurgence: (1), the world's increased demand for energy; (2) a highly educated citizenry. "In an age where human capital is a far greater predictor of national vitality than raw population numbers, the quality of Russia's people can and likely will, outweigh any issues with quantity;" (3), technological breakthroughs in the military sphere; (4), Russia's "position to ally with a wider range of powers than any other state." Dibb, "The Bear is Back," 78.

11. Parker, "Inside the 'Collapsing' Soviet Economy," 74.

12. Yergin & Gustafson, *Russia 2010*, 169.

13. Anders Åslund, "Russia's Success Story," *Foreign Affairs* (September/October 1994). See also, "Under New Management," *The Economist*, 18 October 1994. What was true in 1994 is even more so today (2008) with the Russian economy expanding at a rate of 5 to 7 percent per annum.

14. Terri Morrison, Wayne A. Conway and Joseph Douress, *Dunn and Broadstreet's Guide to Doing Business Around the World* (Englewood Cliffs, NJ: Prentice Hall, 1997). 34f.; 57f.; 106f.; 187f.; 299f.; 346f.; 413f.; 423.

15. Barbara Peitsch, *Russia Review*, 30 January 1998, p. 46.

16. "Eastern Europe Recasts Itself: A Survey of Business in Eastern Europe," *The Economist*, 22-28 November 1997, 4-22; p. 62f.

17. Neela Banerjee, "A Look Back at 1997," *Russia Review*, 30 January 1998, p. 9.

18. Guy Chagin, "Russian Economy May Be Recovering," *Wall Street Journal*, 2 November 2005, p. A3.

19. Andrew Kramer, "Awash in Petrodollars, Russia Frets About the Paradoxes of Bounty," *New York Times*, 15 November 2005, pp. C1, C4; Gregory L. White, "Putin Moves to Kick-Start Agenda," *Wall Street Journal*, 15 November 2005, pp. A20, A21.

20. Stiglitz, *The Roaring Nineties*, 229, 230. Also by the same author, *Making Globalization Work* (New York: W.W. Norton & Co., 2006), 16, 17.

21. Logue, Plekhanov & Simmons, A Second Revolution from Above," in *Transforming Russian Enterprises*, 262.

22. Ibid.

23. Christopher L. Slater, Joseph J. Hobbs, *et.,al.*, *Essentials of World Regional Geography*, 2nd ed., (Orlando, FL: Harcourt, Brace College Publishing, 1995), 185; also, W. Bruce Lincoln, *The Conquest of A Continent: Siberia and the Russians* (New York: Random House, 1994), 226; Benson Bobrick, *East of the Sun: The Epic Conquest and Tragic History of Siberia* (New York: Henry Holt & Co., Inc., 1992).

24. Billington sees Siberia not only as "a great repository of natural resources, but also as an emerging transportation bridge between Europe and Asia. Academic and governmental officials," he continues, "suggest that Siberia has the potential to provide (1) an extended European land link with East Asia by improving the Trans-Siberian Railway and building a parallel East-West highway for trucking. (2) shorter air routes between South Asia and North America by opening new channels and airports for transpolar flights." Billington, *Russia in Search of Itself*, 115.

25. Slater, Hobbs, et. al., *Essentials of World Regional Geography*, 187. Mike Tidewell, founder and director of the U.S. Climate Emergency Council, writes pessimistically of global warming and its deleterious impact on the Arctic: "Just since 1979, satellite data show that roughly 250 million acres of perennial sea ice has vanished. That's a loss equal to subtracting from the lower forty-eight states an area five times the size the state of New Jersey. In 2005, we saw the biggest decline yet. Seventy million acres of sea ice gone in one year. That's another New England plus New York state in twelve months." Mike Tidewell, *The Ravaging Tide* (New York: The Free Press, 2006), 57. Be that as it may, the NSR, or North Sea Route, writes Scott G. Borgerson, International Affairs Fellow at the Council of Foreign Relations, "would reduce the sailing distance between Rotterdam and Yokohama from 11,200 nautical miles-via the current route through the Suez Canal-to only 6,500 nautical miles, a savings of more than 40 percent." Currently, "[a] fast lane is now under development" which will take ships directly across a projected ice-free North Pole during the summer months from the Arctic port of Murmansk in Russia to the Hudson Bay port of Churchill, in Canada, "which is connected to the North American rail network." Arctic routes, claims Borgerson, "would force further competition between the Panama and Suez Canals, thereby reducing current canal toles; shipping checkpoints such as the Strait of Malacca would no longer dictate global shipping patterns; and the Arctic seaways would allow for greater international economic integration." Global warming, Borgerson points out, "has given birth to a new scramble for territory and resources..." in the Arctic. Among the five so called, "Arctic powers," Russia, he writes, "was the first to stake its claim" when, in 2001, "Moscow submitted a claim to the United Nations for 460,000 square miles of resource-rich Arctic waters..." known as the Lomonsov Ridge which Russia claims "is a natural extension of the Eurasian landmass" extending into the Arctic Ocean from Siberia. Ignoring the UN's rejection of this "ambitious annexation," in August 2007, Russia "nevertheless dispatched a nuclear-power icebreaker and two submarines to plant its flags on the North Pole's sea floor." The largest deposits of oil and gas are located in the Arctic adjacent to the far northern Russian coastline. The Russian Ministry of Natural Resources, "calculates that the territory claimed by Moscow could contain as much as 586 billion barrels of oil-although these deposits are unproven. By comparison, all of Saudi Arabia's current proven oil reserves amount to only 260 billion barrels," excluding "unexplored and speculative resources..." Scott B. Borgerson, "Arctic Meltdown: The Economic and Security Implications of Global Warming," *Foreign Affairs* (March/April 2008): 63-77.

26. Slater et. al., *Essential of World Regional Geography*, 179. The "Slavic Coreland" contains most of Russia's Slavic population and extends from the Black and Baltic Seas to the region around Novosibirsk in Siberia. Besides Russia (the largest part of the "Coreland,"), Belarus, Moldavia, Ukraine, and northern Kazakhstan also fall within it. Areas outside the "Coreland" are a storehouse of minerals, timber and waterpower which makes it essential that Russia control them.

27. Dimitry Trenin, *The End of Eurasia: Russia on the Border Between Geopolitics and Globalization* (Washington, D.C. & Moscow: Carnegie Endowment for International Peace, 2002), 305, 306.

28. Billington, *Russia in Search of Itself*, 108, 109.

29. Russia, since the dissolution of the Soviet Union, writes geographer Dennis J.B. Shaw, "is no longer a superpower, yet it can hardly avoid being a great one. The largest country in the world, with a population and vast resources, it spans the Northern Hemisphere. Russia has a geographical presence in two of the world's great oceans, overlooks the Arctic and looms to the north of the Middle East. This unique geopolitical position," Shaw concludes, not only "virtually guarantees Russia influence over world affairs...it

also guarantees that the world will be interested in Russian ones." Dennis J.B. Shaw, *Russia in the Modern World: A New Geography*, 287.

Postscript

A New Cold War? Russia, the West and the "Near Abroad"

Russia's recent assertiveness has provoked fears among many observers of the Russian scene that a new Cold War may be at hand. Should this come to pass, most Russia analysts agree that the most probable arena of conflict will be the ex-Soviet states of Russia's "Near Abroad." At issue here is the quest for energy security. The world has entered the era of what *Asia Times* journalist, Pepe Escobar, calls "pipeline power, where geopolitical turmoil is intimately linked to gas-pipeline routes, as in the Northern European Gas Pipeline, the Russo-German project under the Baltic Sea (bypassing the Baltic states and Poland), the pipeline from Venezuela to Argentina via Brazil, bypassing Bolivia."[1] The main weapon in this potential East-West confrontation is the manipulation of natural gas supplies, of which Russia is currently the world's largest producer. "[A]t a time when the West [primarily the U.S.] is increasingly preoccupied [with the wars in Iraq and Afghanistan], Russia," write reporters Marc Champion and Guy Chazan, "has scored big gains and is taking off the gloves."[2]

In the battle for influence and energy, Georgia, Ukraine, and the post-Soviet states of Central Asia are the central focus of controversy. Here, Putin "has defended," comments *The Economist*, "what he sees as Russia's interest with ruthless pragmatism."[3] In late 2006, in response to Georgia's arrest of four Russian military officers on spy charges, Moscow imposed a strict embargo on trade and transport, "akin to the U.S. embargo on Cuba" in order to apply pressure to Georgia's pro-Western government. During a presidential phone conversation between Putin and Bush on the matter, Putin's implied message was emphatic: "Don't interfere!" Despite the presence of American troops and a government in Tbilisi, the Georgian capital, that is decidedly pro-Western, Moscow "appears to have read the spy dispute as a sign that the West's willingness to intervene is limited."[4]

In an attempt to force Ukraine to pay the higher market price for natural gas (previously supplied at subsidized rates), Russia's gas giant, Gazprom, on New Year's Day 2006, curtailed deliveries. It also began reducing pressure on transmission lines carrying supplies through Ukraine to Western Europe which purchases a quarter (25%) of its natural gas from Russia (as was noted in a previous chapter.) Ukraine, in turn, siphoned off some of the diminished supply, provoking fears among Western Europeans that an energy crisis would result at the start of winter. "Although emphasizing the price issue," writes Michael T. Klare, professor of peace and world security studies at Hampshire College, "Russian officials apparently intended to constrict Ukraine's energy supplies as a way of punishing that country's pro-Western president, Viktor Yushchenko, architect of the Orange revolution, for his ventures to NATO and the EU."[5] Whatever the case, by the end of January, Russia had restored the flow of natural gas to Western and to Central Europe, after Ukraine, albeit reluctantly, agreed to pay the higher price demanded by Russia.

In Central Asia, the former Soviet republic of Uzbekistan, ejected U.S. military bases put there in the aftermath of 9/11, while it has been strengthening security and other attachments to Russia. In August 2006, Uzbekistan joined the Russia-led Collective Security Treaty Organization (CSTO), described as "a Russian project that aims to exclude membership in other security alliances, particularly NATO."[6] CSTO was created in May 2003, comprised of Russia, Kazakhstan, Kyrgyzstan, Tajikistan, Belarus and Armenia, as a collective security organization headquartered in Moscow. It was designed, writes historian Philip Longworth, as "a rapid-reaction force for Central Asia under Russian command and [as] a common defense system. [Member states] also agreed to co-ordinate foreign policy and security."[7] Under the terms of the treaty, Russia also acquired "a permanent lease on a military air-base at Kant in Kyrgyzstan, at the heart of the region and within range of Afghanistan, Pakistan, India and China."[8]

The Collective Security Treaty Organization can be seen as a counterpoint to GUUAM (the acronym for Georgia, Uzbekistan—no longer a member— Ukraine, Azerbaijan, and Moldova), created in 1997, "ostensibly," says Escobar , "to 'favor economic multilateral cooperation,' but really as a regional military alliance under the protection of NATO, strategically placed right on the path of the Caspian Sea's energy wealth." In point of fact, GUUAM, states Escobar emphatically, "was an anti-Moscow club."[9] GUUAM may have been what Putin had in mind when, at the 43rd Munich Conference on Security Policy, held in February 2007, he accused the United States of "provoking a new nuclear arms race by developing ballistic missile defenses, undermining international institutions [i.e., the UN], and making the Middle East more unstable through its clumsy handling of the Iraq war." He was especially critical of the work of foreign organizations (NGOs) based in Russia to assist democratization, accusing them of being used, "as channels for funding...by governments of other countries" which are "hidden from our society...This is about one country [an oblique reference to the U.S.] influencing another."[10]

Significantly, GUUAM's headquarters is located in Kiev, Ukraine's capital, which, since the Orange revolution, "has become a defacto 'alternative integration center.'" In the words of the Russian daily, *Kommersant*, GUUAM is searching for "'an alternative to Gazprom.'" One possible alternative to Russian sources of energy is the Baku-Tbilisi-Erzurum (BTE) gasoduct "which runs parallel to the Baku-Tbilisi-Ceyhan (ETC) oil pipeline, reaching Turkey and the European markets," thereby bypassing Russia altogether.

At the Geopolitics of Energy Security seminar held in Brussels, Russia pressed the EU to define what the seminar's main theme, "diversification of energy supply" actually means, especially where Russia is concerned. The EU fears that Russia intends to use natural gas as a political weapon, while the Russians, for their part, see energy supply diversification as another way to pressure Russia and which could, potentially, result in the loss of traditional Russian exports to the West. Currently, the EU is actively engaged in talks with both Kazakhstan and Turkmenistan—and also with Iran—in the attempt to bypass Russia via the south Caucasus and the Caspian Sea. "The key project in this Pipelinestan mode," writes Escobar, "is the proposed Trans-Caspian gasoduct—which would, in effect, break Russia's monopoly on transit of Central Asian gas," a prospect hardly welcomed by Russia.[11]

At the center of the controversy over energy security in Russia's "Near Abroad," is Gazprom whose goal is to become "a global gas giant under vertical integration, selling gas to everyone and his neighbor." Gazprom's ultimate objective, we are told, "is to control the whole chain—from production to the final consumer in Europe." The EU, on the other hand, wants Gazprom "to bring gas to the EU's borders, where [it] will be bought by EU partners who will then distribute it inside Europe."[12] Such an arrangement, however, could put an end to the highly favorable long-term contracts Gazprom has with European energy giants, a prospect which Russia finds unacceptable.

Anxious to complete the construction of the $4.8 billion Northern European Pipeline, the planned Russo-German gasoduct under the Baltic Sea, Russia and Germany have formed an energy alliance comprising Gazprom and the main German energy companies, E.ON and BASF. Former German Chancellor, Gerhard Schroeder, was placed at the head of the supervisory board of the Russo-German consortium and given the task of supervising the building the undersea pipeline. E.ON and BASF were allotted 24.5 percent of shares each. Besides the Baltic Sea gasoduct, Gazprom is attempting to purchase additional gasoducts and distribution companies in Europe, such as British Centrica, a move which was blocked by opposition from the British government.

Emboldened by its newfound assertiveness, "the Kremlin," comments *The Economist*, "is now as eager to be feared as liked," which is most likely why Putin feels that Russia can strenuously object to America's proposed missile-defense plan.[13] To counteract what it perceives as the U.S. drive to control the world's energy sources, Russia is actively seeking "to invest in a strategic energy partnership with the EU."[14] The abovementioned Russo-German gasoduct may very well be part of that goal. When Putin visited the Middle East in mid-February 2007, "he again talked mischievously about setting up a 'gas OPEC.'" It may also explain why, at the Munich Conference, he asserted that "Russia did not lose the Cold War, but voluntarily ended it."[15] And in an interview with *al-Jazeera*, Putin "again insisted that non-governmental organizations active in Russia but funded from abroad, were tools of foreign governments...," making plain "the basic conviction...that all American talk about Russia's democratic failings was so much realpolitik." Those who criticize Russia's human-rights record, he said, "are using this kind of demagogy as a means to pursue their own foreign-policy goals in Russia."[16]

Russia also recognizes that, as far as long-term energy security is concerned, "the future of global developments in Asia," is primarily in China and India with their rapidly developing economies. In fact, claims Escobar, Russia "is actually in search of a Euro-Asian equilibrium," which may be one more reason for the creation of CSTO. According to Natalia Narotchitskaia, vice president of the Russian Duma Commission of Foreign Affairs, Russia's greatest advantage in terms of the energy security issue is that it can boast of "energy independence, military power, high levels of education, a complete cycle of scientific research, no overpopulation, a huge territory, and a modest level of consumption." Indeed, she declares, Russia currently is "[t]he only country in the world to meet these criteria..." In practical terms, she continues, "this should translate into more investment to explore Eastern Siberia and the Russian Far East" without the necessity of integration "either with the EU or with NATO." Instead, Narotchitskaia favors a true "independent historical project." Energy security, to her, means "a geoeconomy which would lift [Russia] from demographic decline, reinforce the country and [attract] our neighbors, especially those in Central Asia."[17]

Preoccupied with the wars in Iraq and Afghanistan, the United States, for its part, appears reluctant to confront Russia directly over the energy security issue. Washington relies on the Kremlin's cooperation as a go-between in disputes with Iran and North Korea over nuclear weapons. Reliance on Russian energy by the U.S. and the EU "has given the Kremlin confidence to risk trying to restore its status in the post-Soviet space," comments Dimitry Ragozon, who is described as "an influential Russian nationalist lawmaker."[18] In his phone conversation with President Bush concerning Georgia, Putin "underlined [in his words] 'the unacceptability and danger of any actions by third nations [an oblique reference to the U.S.] that could be interpreted by the Georgian leadership as an encouragement of its destructive policy.'"[19] In early October 2006, during a meeting with parliamentary leaders in Moscow, Putin even raised the possibility of Russia's recognizing the independence of South Ossetia and Abkhazia, two breakaway regions of Georgia which have been under the control of Russian-supported separatists since the early 1990s. "If NATO wants Georgia at any price," warns Sergei Barburin, the deputy speaker of the Russian State Duma, "then it can have it without Abkhazia and [South] Ossetia." There are some observers who are deeply concerned that a confrontation between Georgia and Russia over these breakaway regions could lead to a wider war, "although both Georgian and Russian officials say that [this] is highly unlikely," at least for the time being.[20]

What can the West do in relation to the "Near Abroad" about a resurgent Russia? "The short answer," comments *The Economist*, "is not a lot." Unless the price of oil unexpectedly collapses to below $20 per barrel, the leverage that was available to the West in the 1990s when "an economically enfeebled Russia needed help from abroad," has virtually disappeared. "With the Kremlin once again firmly in control, Russia will only change from within," concludes *The Economist*, glumly, "or not at all."[21] All things considered, one fact is certain:

Russia, argues Dimitry Trenin of the Carnegie Moscow Center, "has now left the Western solar system and is busily creating its own." What this portends for the future of East-West relations, only time will tell.[22]

Notes

1. Pepe Escobar, "The Gazprom nation," *Asia Times*, http://www.atimes.com/atimes/central-asia/He 26 Agagoi.html 26 May 2006. The disputed Balkan territory of Kosovo is another area of possible conflict between Washington and Moscow. Russian deputy foreign minister Vladimir Titov, in late April 2007, issued a warning to Martii Ahtissari, the UN envoy, that the plan he had prepared for supervised independence for Kosovo and endorsed by the U.S., Britain, and other EU members, could be vetoed by Russia should it come before the Security Council. Writes journalist Stefan Wagstyl: "[W]ith Moscow keen to demonstrate its political resurgence, Kosovo is an opportunity to assert Russia's influence deep in Europe," adding that, "[t]he Kremlin still resents the 1999 NATO assault which forced Serbia [a traditional ally and a Balkan base for Russian companies], from Kosovo." Stefan Wagstyl, "Moscow Issues a Warning Over Kosovo," (World News), *Financial Times*, 27 April 2007, p.2. For Russia and the "Near Abroad," see, Dimitry Simes, "America and the Post-Soviet Republics," *Foreign Affairs* (Summer 1992): 73-89; in the same issue, Adrian Karatnycky, "the Ukrainian Factor:" 90-107; Martha Brill Olcott, "Central Asia's Catapult to Independence:" 108-130; Dawisha and Parott, *Russia and the New States of Eurasia*, Chapter 5, 186-192. For relations between Russia and Ukraine, see, Igor Torbakov, "Apart from Russia or Part of Russia: A Sad Saga of Russian-Ukrainian Relations," *Demokratizatsiya*, 9:4 (Fall 2001): 588-602. For the beginnings of the energy security issue, see Edward L. Morse and James Richard, "The Battle for Energy Dominance," *Foreign Affairs* (March/April 2002): 16-31; David G. Victor and Nadjda M. Victor, "Axis of Oil," *Foreign Affairs* (March/April 2003): 47-61.

2. Marc Champion and Guy Chazan, "Moscow Trumps the West in Battle for Clout in Former Soviet States," *Wall Street Journal*, 6 October 2006, pp. A1, A10.

3. "Richer, Bolder and Sliding Back," *The Economist* (Special Report: Russia), 15 July 2006, p. 25.

4. Champion & Chazan, "Moscow Trumps the West," p. A10. This was made clearly evident by the indecisiveness of the U.S. and EU response to the Russian invasion of Georgia in August 2008.

5. Michael T. Klare, "The Geopolitics of Natural Gas," *The Nation*, 23 January 2006, p. 18.

6. Champion & Chazan, "Moscow Trumps the West," p. A10.

7. Philip Longworth, *Russia: The Once and Future Empire from Pre-History to Putin* (New York: St. Martin's Press, 2006), 325, 326.

8. Champion & Chazan, "Moscow Trumps the West," p. A10. Here, one is tempted to speculate whether the alliance of former Soviet Central-Asian republics and Russia can be seen as a catalyst for the "reintegration" of the old Soviet Union, a desired goal of many Russian nationalists today. Be that as it may, there can be little doubt that Russia's policy in Central Asia, coupled with the Middle East and China, is part of a larger strategy for great-power if not superpower status.

9. Escobar, "The Gazprom Nation."

10. Thom Shanker and Mark Lindler, "Putin Say U.S. is Undermining Global Stability," *New York Times*, 11 February 2007, pp. A1, A4.

11. Escobar, "The Gazprom Nation."

12. Ibid. "Gazprom's swagger," comments *Business Week*, "reflects more than the company's muscle abroad. The assertiveness also points to Gazprom's ascendancy as Russia's preeminent economic institution and as a central player in domestic politics." Gazprom alone, we are told, "generates 8 percent of natural gas revenues, while the broader energy sector provides the main thrust lifting per capita income in Russia by about 10 percent a year." Jason Bush and Anthony Bianco, "Why Russians Love Gazprom No Matter What the World Thinks," *Business Week*, 31 July 2006, p. 37.

13. "Not a Cold War, But a Cold Tiff," *The Economist*, 17 February 2007, p. 61. In his final state-of-the-nation address on April 26, 2007, Putin, in protest of the U.S. proposed anti-missile system to be based in Poland and the Czech Republic, "announced a moratorium on Russian observance of the 1990 Conventional Forces in Europe Treaty, which imposes limits on non-nuclear weapons in Europe," threatening to withdraw Russia "from the treaty altogether unless NATO countries ratified a revised version agreed to in 1999." All this occurred despite an invitation by the U.S. to Russia to share missile defense technology and operate radar sites jointly. Many Europeans, write reporters Thom Shanker and Mark Landler, fear that the harsh exchanges between Russia and the U.S. "will knock the lid off the ash bin of Cold War history," and constitute "the latest example of how the U.S. and Russia say they want to work together but talk past each other." Thom Shanker and Mark Landler, "Europe Worries as Russia and the U.S. Argue Over Missiles," *New York Times*, 28 April 2007, p. A3. Also, Neil Buckley and Daniel Dombey, "Putin Makes Threat on Arms Treaty," (World News), *Financial Times*, 27 April 2007, p.2.

14. Escobar, "The Gazprom Nation."

15. "Not a Cold War, But a Cold Tiff," p. 61.

16. Ibid.

17. Escobar, "The Gazprom Nation." Taking Narotchitskaia's observations at face value we can perhaps detect the vague outlines of the "Slavic-Turkic union" envisioned by Eurasianists and grounded on what Escobar calls "the Gazprom nation." Although a segment of contemporary Russian nationalism is stridently anti-Muslim, the idea of an entente between Russian Muslims and modern Russian nationalism continues to exert great appeal. Several figures of Muslim-Tartar background, we are told, are in accord with their fellow Eurasianists and comments *The Economist*, "subscribe to the ideal of a Eurasian or 'Slavic-Turkic' union—roughly coinciding with the Soviet Union—whose common enemy is global or Anglo-Saxon [read _eoliberals] capitalism." In the Kremlin's calculations, "[t]he attractions of a concordat between Russian nationalists and Muslims are still a factor." Muslim leaders in Russia, such as the mufti, Talgat Tajuddin, who met with Putin in July 2006, have signaled that they are "ready to line up with conservative Russian nationalists against things they all dislike," including American policy. "Mosque and State," *Economist*, 15 July 2006, pp. 80, 81.

18. Champion & Chazan, "Moscow Trumps the West," p. A10.

19. Ibid.

20. Ibid. In fact, Russia did eventually recognize the independence both of Abkhazia and South Ossetia following the ill-fated attach by Georgia on the South Ossetian capital on August 7, 2008 which was decisively repulsed by Russian troops. For the most recent reaction to the so called, Five-Day War, see articles by Charles King, "The Five-Day War," and Stephen Sestanovich, "What Has Moscow Done?" in *Foreign Affairs* (November/December 2008): 2-28.

21. "Living With a Strong Russia," *The Economist*, 15 July 2006, p. 9. Fear of what many Russian officials have labeled a "creeping coup" analogous to the Orange revolution in Ukraine, has prompted Putin to crack down on those NGOs (non-governmental organizations) operating in Russia which he considers suspicious or untrustworthy. In his state-of-the-nation speech to the Duma, Putin warned, writes reporter Alan Cullison, "that Russia's opponents are using 'pseudemocratic slogans' to return the country to chaos," declaring that "'there is a growing stream of money from abroad being used to directly interfere in our internal affairs.'" Alan Cullison, "Putin to Keep Political Reigns Tight," *Wall Street Journal*, 27 April 2007, p. A10.

22. "Living With a Strong Russia," p. 9. Increased global trade and commerce means greater economic integration by Russia with Europe and the U.S. This overall fact decreases the likelihood of confrontation. No matter what their disagreements, both Russia and the U.S. have too much at stake economically to risk upsetting the status quo. This, in turn, has created a new economic dynamic which is currently changing the balance of power between Russia and the West.

Bibliography

Newspaper and Magazines
The following publications are for 1990-2008

Atlantic Monthly
Aviation Week & Space Technology
Business Week
Delovie Lyudi
Detroit Free Press
Detroit News
The Economist
Financial Times
The Nation
The New Republic
New York Times
Russian Conservation News
Russian Life
Russia Review
Wall Street Journal

Books, Journals, and Conference Papers

Adler, Mortimer, *Haves Without Have Nots: Essays for the Twenty-First Century on Democracy and Socialism*. New York: Macmillan Publishing Co., 1991.
Ashford, Robert, Rodney Shakespeare. *Binary Economics: The New Paradigm*. New York: University Press of America, 1999.
Aslund, Anders. "Russia's Success Story," *Foreign Affairs* (September/October 1994).
_____. *How Russia Became a Market Economy*. Washington D.C.: The Brookings Institute, 1995.
_____. *Building Capitalism: The Transformation of the Former Soviet Bloc*. Cambridge: University Press, 2002.
Bacevich, Andrew. *American Empire: The Reality and the Consequences of U.S. Diplomacy*. Cambridge, MA: Harvard University Press, 2002.
Barner-Barny, and Cynthia A. Hody. *The Politics of Change: The Transformation of the Former Soviet Union*. New York: St. Martin's Press, 1995.
Bello, Waldo. *Dilemmas of Domination: The Unmaking of the American Empire*. New York: Henry Holt & Co., 2005.
Billington, James. *Russia in Search of Itself*. Baltimore & London: The Johns Hopkins University Press, 2004.
Bird, Kai, Martin J. Sherwing. *American Prometheus: The Triumph and Tragedy of J. Robert Oppenheimer*. New York: Alfred A. Knopf, 2005.
deBlij, Harm. *Why Geography Matters: Three Challenges Facing America*. Oxford: University Press, 2005.

Blasi, Joseph R., Maya Kroumova and Douglas Kruse. *Kremlin Capitalism: Privatizing the Russian Economy.* Ithaca, NY: Cornell University Press, 1997.
Bobrick, Benson. *East of the Sun: Epic Conquest and Tragic History.* New York: Henry Holt & Co., Inc., 1992.
Boyco, Maxim, Andrei Schliefer and Robert Vishny. *Privatizing Russia.* Cambridge MA: The MIT Press, 1995.
Brady, Rose. *Kapitalizm: Russia's Struggle to Free its Economy.* New Haven: Yale University Press, 1999.
Committee for Social & Economic Justice Mission to Moscow. *The Economic Justice Monitor* (Newsletter of the Center for Economic & Social Justice) 12:1 (Summer 1997).
Chubarov, Alexander. *The Fragile Empire: A History of Imperial Russia.* New York: Continuum, 1999.
Clover, Charles. "Dreams of the Eurasian Heartland: The Reemergance of Geopolitics" *Foreign Affairs* 78:2 (March/April 1999): 9-13.
Cosimo, J.C. "Warming Trends in the Arctic from Clear Sky Observations." *Journal of Climate* 15 (2003).
Dawisha, Karen and Bruce Parott. *Russia and the New States of Eurasia: The Politics of Upheaval.* Cambridge: University Press, 1994.
Deutscher, Isaac. *Stalin: A Biography.* New Edition. New York: Vintage Books, 1960.
Djelic, Bozidar. "Mass Privatization in Russia: The Role of Vouchers." *RFE/RL Research Project* 1, October 16, 1992, 40-44.
Dobb, Maurice. *Soviet Economic Development Since 1917.* New York: International Publishers, 1948.
Donald M., and John Logue, eds. *Transitions to Capitalism and Democracy in Russia and Central Europe: Achievements, Problems, Prospects.* Westview CT: Praeger, 2000.
Dunlop, John R. *The Rise of Russia and the Fall of the Soviet Union.* Princeton, NJ: Princeton University Press, 1993.
Estrin, Saul. Ed. *Privatization in Central and Eastern Europe.* New York: Longman, 1994.
Figis, Orlando. *Natasha's Dance: A Cultural History of Russia.* New York: Henry Holt & Co., 2002.
Freeland, Chrystia. *Sale of the Century: Russia's Wild Ride from Communism to Communism.* New York: Crown Business, 2000.
Garrison, Jim. *American Empire: Global Leader or Rogue Power.* San Francisco: Berrett-Koehler Publications, INC., 2004.
Gates, Jeff. "Global Application of Employee Ownership." *The Journal of Employee Law and Finance* 7 (Fall 1995): 445-459.
_____. *The Ownership Solution: Toward a Shared Capitalism for the Twenty-First Century.* Reading, MA: Addison-Wesley, 1998.
Goldman, Marshall I. *What Went Wrong with Perestroika?* New York: W.W. Norton Norton & Co., 1992.
Gorbachev, Mikhail. *Perestroika: New Thinking for Our Country and the World.* New York: Harper & Row, 1987.
Greider, William. *The Soul of Capitalism: Opening Paths to a Moral Economy.* New York: Simon & Schuster, 2003.
Gustafson, Thane. *Capitalism Russian-Style.* Cambridge: University Press, 1997.

Bibliography

Hancock, Donald and John Logue, eds. *Transitions to Capitalism and Democracy in Russia and Central Europe: Achievements, Problems, Prospects.* Westport, CT: Greenwood Press, 2000.

Hanson, Philip. *The Rise and Fall of the Soviet Economy: An Economic History of the USSR from 1945.* London: Longman, 2003.

Hassol, S.J. *Impacts of a Warming Arctic: Arctic Climate Impact Assessment.* Cambridge: University Press, 2004.

Hewett, Edward A. *Reforming the Soviet Economy.* Washington, D.C.: The Brookings Institution, 1988.

Higgins, Michael and David Binns. "The Role of Employee Ownership in Russian Privatization." Paper presented to the Foundation for Enterprise Development, Bonn, Germany, August 10-13, 1994.

Hill, Fiona and Florence Fee. "Fueling the Future: The Prospects for Russian Oil and Gas." *Demokratizatsiya* 10:4 (Fall 2002): 475.

Hoffman, David. *The Oligarchs: Wealth and Power in the New Russia.* New York: Public Affairs, 2002.

Hough, Jerry R. *Democratization and Revolution in the USSR, 1985-1991.* Washington D.C.: The Brookings Institution, 1998.

Huntington, Samuel P. *The Clash of Civilizations and the Remaking of the World Order.* New York: Simon & Schuster, 1996.

Jack, Andrew. *Inside Putin's Russia.* Oxford: The University Press, 2004.

Kaljic, Matthew, A. ed. *The Breakup of Communism.* New York: H.W. Wilson & Co., 1993.

Karasik, Theodore. "Putin and Shoigu: Reversing Russia's Decline." *Demokratizatsiya* 8 (Spring 2000): 178-185.

Kelso, Louis with Mortimer Adler. *The Capitalist Manifesto.* New York: Random House, 1958.

_____. "The Almost Capitalist." *The American Bar Association Journal* 43 (March 1957): 235-279.

_____. with Mortimer Adler. *The New Capitalists.* New York: Random House, 1961.

_____. with Patricia Hetter Kelso. *Democracy and Economic Power: Extending the ESOP Revolution through Binary Economics.* Lanham, MD: University Press, 1986, 1991.

Kennedy, Paul. *The Rise and Fall of the Great Powers.* New York: Random House, 1987.

Keylor, William. *The Twentieth-Century World: An International History.* New York and Oxford: Oxford University Press, 1984.

Keremetsky, Jacob and John Logue. *Perestroika, Privatization and Worker Ownership in the USSR.* Kent, OH: Popular Press, 1991.

Kokh, Alfred. *The Selling of the Soviet Empire: Politics & Economics of Russia's Privatization—Revelations of a Political Insider.* Translated from the Russian text. New York: S.P.I. Books, 1998.

Klebnikov, Paul. *Godfather of the Kremlin: Boris Berezovsky and the Looting of Russia.* New York: Harcourt, 2000.

Kurland, Norman, Dawn K. Brohawn and Michael Greaney. *Capital Homesteading for Every Citizen: A Just Free Market Solution for Saving Social Security.* Washington, D.C.: Economic Justice Media, 2004.

Kvint, Vladimir. *The Barefoot Shoemaker: Capitalizing on the New Russia.* New York: Arcade Press, 1993.

_____. "Don't Give Up on Russia." *Harvard Business Review* (March/April 1994).

Lawrence, Paul and Charalimbos Veachoutsicos. "Joint Ventures in Russia: Put the Locals in Charge." *Harvard Business Review* (January/February 1993): 44-54.

Layard, Richard and John Parker. *The Coming Russian Boom: A Guide to Markets and Politics.* New York: The Free Press, 1996.

Liebermann, Ira and John Ellis. Ed. Russia: *Creating Private Enterprises, Efficient Enterprises and Efficient Markets.* Washington, D.C: The World Bank: The Private Sector Development Department, 1994.

_____. And Shuail Rahija. "An Overview of Mass Privatization in Russia." Working paper presented to the World Bank Conferences, Washington, D.C., June 20, 21, 1994.

Lincoln, W. Bruce. *The Conquest of a Continent: Siberia and the Russians.* New York: Random House, 1994.

Logue, John and Dan Bell. "Worker Ownership in Russia: A Possiblity after the Command Economy." *Dissent* (Spring 1992): 199-204.

_____. John Simmons and Sergei Plekhanov, eds. *Transforming Russian Enterprises: From State Control to Employee Ownership.* Westport, CT: The Greenwood Press, 1995.

Mackinder, H.J. "The Geographical Pivot of History." *Geographical Journal* 23 (1904).

Mares, Derek, ed. The *History of Nations: Russia.* Farmington Hills, MI: Greenhaven Press, 2003.

Meier, Andrew. *Black Earth: A Journey through Russia after the Fall.* New York: W.W. Norton & Co., 2003.

Mitsek, Sergey. "The State of Employee Ownership in Russia." *The Journal of Employee Ownership Law and Finance.* 10 (Fall 1998): 135-139.

Mobius, Mark. *Passport to Profits.* New York: Warner Books, 1999.

Morrison, Terri, Wayne Conway and Joseph J. Douress. *Dun & Broadstreet's Guide to Doing Business Around the World.* Englewood Cliffs, NJ: Prentice Hall, 1997.

Nelson, Kynn D. and Irina Y. Kuzes. *Property to the People: The Struggle for Radical Economic Reform in Russia.* Zrmonk, NY: M.E. Sharpe, 1994.

Nichols, Thomas. *The Russian Presidency: Society and Politics in the Second Russian Republic.* New York: Palgrave, 1999.

Nove, Alec. *An Economic History of the USSR.* New York: Pelican Books, 1972.

Parker, Richard. *John Kenneth Gailbraith: His Life, His Politics, His Economics.* New York: Farrar, Straus & Giroux, 2005.

Piveronus, Jr. Peter J. "Direct Worker Ownership: The Russian Formula for Economic Reform." *Essays in Economic & Business History* 27 (1999): 255.

_____. *The Reinvetion of Capitalism: Russia's Alternative to Corporate Concentration and to the Command Economy.* Lewiston, NY: The Edwin Mellen Press, 2006.

Pomper, Philip. *The Russian Revolutionary Intellgensia.* Arlington Heights. IL: Davidson, Inc., 1970.

Posner, Vladimir. *Parting with Illusions: The Extraordinary Life and Controversial Views of the Soviet Union's Leading Commentator.* New York: The Atlantic Monthly Press, 1990.

Primakov, Ye. M. *The East after the Collapse of the Colonial System.* Moscow: Nauka Publishing House, 1983.

Simes, Dimitri. "America and the Post-Soviet Republics." *Foreign Affairs* 71 (Summer 1992): 73-89.

Bibliography

Shnirman, Viktor and Sergei Panarin. "Lev Gumilev: His Pretensions as a Founder of Ethnology and His Eurasian Theories." *Inner Asia* 3 (2000).

Sivyachev, N.V. and N.N. Yakovlev. *Russia and the United States: U.S.-Soviet Relations from the Soviet Point of View*. Olgar Adler Titelbaum, trans. Chicago: The University of Chicago Press, 1979.

Slater, Christopher L., Joseph Hobbes, et. al. *Essentials of World Regional Geography*. 2nd ed. Orlando, FL: Harcourt Brace College Publishing, 1995.

Supyan, Victor. "Privatization in Russia: Preliminary Results and Socioeconomic Implications." *Demokratizatsiya* 9 (Winter 2001): 137-150.

Taylor, A.J.P. *From Sarajevo to Potsdam*. New York: Harcourt, Brace & World, 1966.

Trenin, Dimitry. *The End of Eurasia: Russia on the Border between Geopolitics and Globalization*. Washington D.C. and Moscow: Carnegie Endowment for International Peace, 2002.

Ulam, Adam B. *A History of Soviet Russia*. New York: Praeger Publishers, 1976.

Vinkovetsky, Ilya and Charles Schlacks, Jr. ed. *Exodus to the East: Forebodings and Events: An Affirmation of the Eurasians*. Idyllwild, CA: Charles Schlacks, Jr. Publisher, 2003.

Weast, Spencer R. *The Discovery of Global Warming*. Cambridge, MA: Harvard University Press, 2005.

Wedel, Jannine R. "Rigging the U.S.-Russian Relationship: Harvard, Chubais and the Transidentity Game." *Demokratizatsiya* 7 (Fall 1999): 469-500.

_____. *Collision and Collusion: The Strange Case of Western Aid to Eastern Europe*. New York: Palgrave, 2001.

Weisskopf, Thomas E. "Myths and Realities of Privatization in Russia." *Review of Radical Economics* 26: 32-40.

Werner, Douglas. *A Little Corner of Freedom*. Berkeley, CA: University of California Press, 2002.

World Bank and European Bank for Reconstruction and Development Study Team. "Mass Privatization in Russia." Moscow, 23 March 1992. Unpublished working document.

Yavlinsky, Gregory. "Russia's Phony Capitalism." *Foreign Affairs* 77 (May-June 1998): 67-79.

Yergin, Daniel and Joseph Stanislaw. *The Commanding Heights: The Battle Between Government and the Market Place that is Remaking the Modern World*. New York: Simon & Schuster, 1998.

Index

A

Academy of Labor and Social Relations of the Independent Trade Unions, xviii, xix

Adler, Mortimer, xiv, xx, xxi

Agricultural Adjustment Act (AAA), xii

Alexperov, Vagit, 27

Alyoshin, Boris, 29, 30

American direct investment, 14

AMOCO, 27

Ansel, Paul, 72

Argumenty I Facty, 14

Artyakov, Vladimir, 30

Aryans, 47

Ashford, Robert, xxi

Aslund, Andrus, 3, 12, 23

AT&T, 15

Atlantic-Richfield, 27

"Atlanticists", 43, 49, 64, 67

Atom Stroiexport, 26

August 1998 Crisis, 1, 9, 15, 23, 78

Australia, 39

Australian National University, 57, 79

Azerbaijan, 27, 63, 84

B

Bacevich, Andrew, 2, 7, 59

Baikal-Amur railroad, 73

Baker, James, 51

Baluevsky, Yuri, Col. Gen., 57

Barner-Barry, Carol, 7

Batsanova, Galina, 10, 18

Bell, Dan, xv-xvii, xxi, 15

Berman, Morris, 2, 3, 7

"Big Three", 74

Billington, James, ix, 40, 41, 45-49, 77, 80, 81

Binary economics, viii, xii, xiv-xvii, xix, xxi, 4, 9, 54, 61, 63-65, 70, 74

Bird, Kai, xii, xx

Blasi, Joseph, 15, 20

Bogdanov, Vladimir, 28

Boguchansk hydroelectric dam, 73

Boston Globe, 2

Boston University, 2

Boyco, Maxim, 5, 8

British Isles, 39
British Petroleum (BP), 27

Index

Broad-based capital ownership, xx

Brohawn, Dawn K., xxi, xxii

Brown, Heidi, 55, 59

Buckley, Neil, vii, ix, 24, 33, 34, 66, 89

Bulava missile, 57

BUTEK, xvi, xxi

Butovsky Concern, xvi

C

C.A. & Co., 14

Capitalist Manifesto, xiv, xxi

Caspian Sea, 27, 84, 85

Celeste, Richard, xv

Center for Economic & Social Injustice, xv

Center for International Relations (Boston University), 2

Center for International Relations (Warsaw, Poland), 62

Central Asia corridor, 63

Centrica, 56, 85

Chaadayev, Ptyr, 37, 45

"Champion Companies", 24

Chavez, Hugo, 52-54, 59, 61

Chazan, Guy, 29, 35, 54, 59, 83, 88, 90

Chechnya, 1

Chernomydrin, Viktor, 24

Chevron, 15

China, vii, viii, xi, xii, xx, 2, 7, 27, 32, 39, 42, 44, 48, 49, 55, 63, 69, 71, 72, 74, 76, 79, 84, 86, 88

Chubais, Anatoly, 3, 5, 8, 64, 74

Clinton, Bill, 2, 4, 5, 10

Clover, Charles, ix, 41, 42, 44, 46-49

Cohen, Stephen, 1, 2, 7, 18, 22

Cold War, 2, 6, 7, 39, 43, 44, 46, 51, 56, 57, 69, 83, 85, 89

"Collective private property", xvii

Congress of People's Deputies, 4, 10

"Columbian Exchange", xi, xx

"Co-management Program", 53

Command economy, xiii, 73

"Conventionalities", 52

Corporate concentration, 73

"Crony capitalism", 1

Crosby, Alfred, xi, xx

"Cultural fronts", 69

Czech Republic, 72, 89

D

deBlij, Harm, 78

Deripaska, Oleg, 29

Deutscher, Isaac, xx

Dibb, Paul, 57, 59, 79

Direct worker ownership, xiv, xvi

Dole, Robert, Sen., 10

Donnelly, Matt, vii

Downing, Danielle, 14

Drogalev, Anatoly, xvii, xviii

Dugin, Aleksandr, 41-44, 48, 76

Dunn & Broadstreet, 79

E

Eastern Oil Company, 63

Eastman-Kodak, 15

Economic liberalization, 12 (see also, globalization, neoliberalism)

Economicheskoe chudo (economic miracle), 70, 71, 79

Economist, xii, xvi, 2, 5, 11, 12, 52

Egypt, 27

Elder, Alexander, 28, 33, 34

Elements: Eurasian Survey, 42

"Energy card", 55, 56

Erlanger, Stephen, 10

ESOP (Employee Stock Option Plans), xii

"Eurasian Heartland", ix, 46-49

Eurasianism (also, Eurasianists), viii, 37-39, 41, 44-49, 63-65, 67, 76, 89

European Union, viii, xiii, 49, 56, 69

F

Fast-track formula, 3 (also, "shock therapy")

"Fault line wars", 69

Federal Industry Agency, 29

Federal Law No. 119, 9 (also, People's Enterprise Law)

Ferguson, Niall, xi, xx

Financial Times, vii, ix, 3, 23, 33, 66, 79, 88, 89

First Five Year Plan (1928-1932), xi, xx

Fitch ratings, 73

Ford, 15, 32

Fordham University, 14

Freedman, Michael, 55, 60

Fyodorov, Svyatoslav, xviii (see, RUPE—Russian Union of People's Enterprises)

G

Gaidar, Yegor, 3, 4, 10, 11, 18, 22, 64, 74

Gailbraith, John Kenneth, xii, xiii, xx, xxi, 46, 51, 59, 61

Ganeyev, Mullanne F., xvii

Gazprom, 10, 18, 23-28, 31, 33, 34, 55, 56, 59, 62, 63, 83-85, 88, 89

Gazpromavia, 25

Gazprombank, 26

Garrison, Jim, 52, 59, 61

General Electric, 15, 59

General Motors Corporation, 30

Geographical Journal, 38, 45

Geopolitics, vii, 42, 46, 81, 85, 88

Georgetown University, 23

Germany, ix, 2, 12, 15, 25, 38, 39, 43, 71, 85

Getty Oil, 27

Glasnost, vi

Global economy, 2

Globalization, 2, 3, 45, 51-54

Gorbachev, Mikhail, viii, xii, xv, xx, 7, 10, 41

Gore-Chernomydrin Agreement (1995), 49

Goskomstat, 72

Gradualist policy, 4, 5, 10, 11

Great Depression, xi, xii, xix

Greenhouse, Steven, 18, 22

Grichenko, Nicolay, N., xviii

Group of Eight, vii, 59

Gustafson, Thane, 23, 33, 34, 70, 79

H

Harrington, Samuel, 69

Harvard-AID Project, 4-6

Harvard University, 3-7, 11, 59

Hay, John, 4, 5

Herbert, Douglas, 19, 20

Hewlett-Packard, 15

Hill, Fiona, 62, 63, 67

Hody, Cynthia A., 7

Household consumption, 13

I

IBM, 15

Ignatius, Adi, 19

IMF (Internaitonal Monetary Fund), xix, 3, 4, 18, 22, 51, 52, 73

"Imperial overstretch", 69

India, viii, 42, 44, 47, 63, 69, 74, 76, 84, 86

Income differentials, 14

Industrial production and output, 13, 15

Inflation rate (Russia), 10, 13, 73

Inside ownership, 11

Institute of Philosophy of the Russian Academy of Sciences, 44

"Insular Groups", 39, 49

International joint ventures, 14

J

Japan, viii, xiii, 2, 33, 38, 39, 44, 45, 55, 69-71

Jaspers, Karl, 47

Joint-stock companies, 11, 16

Joseph industries, xv

K

Kaliningrad enclave, 29

Kamaz, 29

Kazakhstan, 27

Kelso, Louis, xii, xiv, xviii, xix, xxi, xxii, 61, 74

Kelso Institute for the Study of Economic Systems, xiv

Kelso, Patricia Hetter, xiv

Kennedy, Paul, 69, 74, 78

Kent State University, xv, xvi, xxi

Khodorkovsky, Mikhail, 31, 35, 55, 73

"Kleptokapitalzm", 6

Kokh, Alfred, 20

Konovalov, Vladimir, 62

Kremlin capitalism, 29

Kurland, Norm, xiv, xv, xvii-xix, xxi

Kuzes, Irina Y., 7, 19

Kvint, Vladimir, 14, 20

L

Layard, Richard, 8, 19, 20, 79

Libya, 27

Liebermann, Ira, 19, 22

Lithuania, 7, 27, 62, 76

Lloyd, John, 3, 7, 33

"Loans-for-shares", 31

Logue, John, xv, xvi, xxi, 7, 21, 66, 80

Lubash, Dan, 14

Lukoil, 27, 34, 59, 62, 63

Lukoil-Baltica, 27

M

Majority-minority Worker ownership, 15, 18, 20

Mackinder, Halford, 37-39, 42, 45-47, 63, 73, 75, 76

Marx, Karl, xv, xx, 75

Mass privatization, xvii, xx, 2-4, 10, 12, 13, 15, 24, 61, 74

MC Securities, 24

Medvedev, Dimitry, 73

Merril-Lynch & Co., Capegemini, 14

Michigan State University, 38, 39, 69

Middle Class (Russia), 19, 20, 34, 66

Miller, Alexei, 24

Mitsek, Sergey, 18

"Mixed economy", 11

Mobius, Mark, 23, 32, 70, 78

"Moscow Consensus", vi, 65

Mosenergo, 26

Mosfumitura, xvi

"Multipolar", 49

N

NAFTA (North American Free Trade Assoc.), 2, 73

"National Strategic Plan", 23, 25

"Natural monopolies", 23, 29, 62

NATO (North Atlantic Treaty Organization), 4, 39, 73, 76, 84, 86, 88, 89

Nazi Germany, xi

Neoliberalism, xiii, 12, 53, 73 (see also, globalization; "Washington Consensus")

New Deal, xii, xix, 35

New Zealand, 39

Nichols, Thomas, 61, 66

Nikonov, Vyacheslav, viii

Northern Sea Route (NSR), 26

Novy-Uregnoy

O

OAO Aeroflot, 29

Ohio Employee Ownership Center (OEOC), xv, xvi, xvii, xxi

Oil & Gas Workers' Union, 28

Oligarchs, 18

Onyszkiewicz, Janusz, 62

Orange Revolution (Ukraine), 59

Ostrovsky, Arkady, ix

Outside ownership, 15

"Ownership economics", xiv

P

Panarin, A.S., 44, 46, 49

Parker, John, xii, xx, xxi, 8, 19, 20, 51, 59, 61, 79

People's Capitalism, 18, 22

People's Enterprise (PE), 9

People's Enterprise Law No. 115, 9

Peitsch, Barbara, 72, 79

Perestroika, viii, xii, xiv, xx, xxi

Perkins, John, 52, 59, 61

Petroleum Advisory Forum, 62

Piveronus, Peter, viii, ix, xx, xxi, 7, 8, 18-22, 33

"Pivot Area", 39

Place-centered enterprises, 26

Platex, 15

Plekhanov, Sergey, xxi, 21, 61, 62, 66, 80

Posner, Vladimir, xi, xix, xx

Poverty rate (Russia), 1, 4

Primakov, Yevgeny, 41, 43, 44, 49

Proto-Indo-European languages, 40

Proto-Slavic-Iranian dialects, 40, 47

Pulpus, 53

Putin, Vladimir, 18, 24-26, 28-30, 35, 49, 51, 54-57, 63, 66, 71, 73, 79, 83-96, 88-90

R

Radical reformers, 3-5

Rahuja, Suhail, 12, 19, 22
Reagan, Ronald, xiii, 2, 51

Index

Renaissance Capital, 27

Robbins, Carla Anne, 7

Rodnyansky, Alexander, viii

Roosevelt, Franklin D., xi, xii

Rosoboronexport, 29, 30

Rosneft, 63

Rosett, Claudia, 19

Rouge Industries, 32, 78 (see also, Severstal)

Royal Geographical Society, 38

"Ruble millionaires", 14

Russian-Chinese Friendship Agreement, 49

Russian Communist Party, 41, 70

Russia's national identity, 37

Russian stock market (RTS), vii, 14, 73

Russian Union of People's Enterprises (RUPE), xviii, xxi

Rutgaizur, Valery M., xvi

Rutgers University, 15

Rutskoi, Aleksandr, 11

S

Sachs, Jeffrey, vii, 3, 6, 11

Salkin, Valery, xviii

Savings rate (Russia), vii, ix

Savitsky, Peter, 39
Seleznev, Gennadi, 42

Severstal, 32, 78 (see also, Rogue Industries)

Shanghai Cooperative Organization, "Shanghai Five", 75

"Shock therapy", 3, 64 (also, neoliberalism)

Siberia, 12, 24, 26-35, 37-38, 66, 73, 74, 80, 81, 86

Sivyackev, Nikolai, xii

Simes, Dimitri, 48, 67, 88

Simmons, John, xxi, 15-17, 20, 21, 66, 80

Slavophile-Westernizer Debate, 37, 38

Sogas, 26

Solovtsov, Nikolai, Gen., 57

Soviet Union, vii, viii, xi-xv, xix, xx, 1, 4, 5, 7, 11, 19, 25, 26, 31, 38, 39, 41, 43, 44, 46, 47, 51, 56, 57, 61, 67, 69, 71, 73, 74, 81, 88, 89

Stalin, Josef, xi, xx, 46

Stanislaw, Joseph, xx, 71, 79

State Committee for the Support and Development of Small Business, 72

Stevenson, Richard, 14, 20

Stiglitz, Joseph, 2, 7, 59, 61, 73, 80

Stockholm Institute of Soviet and East European Economic Affairs, 3

Strategic Enterprise (SE), 18, 23, 25, 28-30

Stroitransgas, 63

Summers, Larry, 63

Supyan, Viktor, 18

Sukhoi Aircraft Corporation, 30

Surgut, 28

Surgutneftgas, 28, 34

Sweden, 4

T

Talbott, Strobe, 4, 5, 7, 8

Templeton Emerging Markets, 70

"Third Wave", 44 (also, "Third Way")

Third World, xiii, 51, 52, 54 (also, Less Developed Countries, LDCs)

Titelbaum, Olga Adler, xx

Topol-M (ICBM), 57

Trade surplus (Russia), 13

Trans-Caucases, 27

Trans-Siberian railroad, 75

"Triumphalism", 2

Trubetskoi, Nikolai, 40, 46, 47

Tuminez, A.S., 43

"Two-Factor Theory", xviii (see also, binary economics)

Tverskoy Meatpacking Plant, xviii

"Turanian East", 41, 65

Tyumen Oblast, 28

U

United Energy System (UES), 26

Ugro-Finns, 41

Ukraine, xx, 26, 42, 56, 59, 66, 75-77, 81, 83, 84, 88, 90

Unemployment (Russia), xiii

United Aircraft Corporation, 30

United States, viii, xi-xiv, xvi, xvii, xx, xxi, 2, 3, 5, 10, 14, 15, 32, 38, 39, 44, 46, 49, 51-53, 56, 57, 61, 69, 70, 71, 73-75, 84, 86

University of California, Berkeley, 3, 5, 8

U.S.-Russia Investment Fund, 72

USSR Council of Ministers, xiv

V

Varvarov, Vlaery, xxi

Venezuela, 48, 52, 54, 83

Volsky, Arkady, 4, 11

Votapek, Vladimir, 56, 59

W

Wall Street Journal, 8, 19, 34, 35, 59, 61, 79, 88, 90

Wanninski, Joseph, 66

"Washington Consensus", viii, 2, 3, 5, 65, 73 (see also, globalization, neo-liberalism)

Washington Times, 1

Wedel, Janine, 3, 5, 7, 8

Weisskopf, Thomas E., 19, 22

Western Europe, 10, 24-26, 43, 44, 55, 56, 64, 72, 74, 75, 83

White, Steven, xix, 7, 41, 79

World Bank, xix, 3, 5, 8, 19, 22, 23, 51, 52, 54, 73

"World Island", 39

Y

Yakovlev, Nikolai, xii, xx, 30

Yanukovich, Viktor, 60

Yale University, 69

Yeltsin, Boris, viii, xv, xvii, xix, 2-4, 10-12, 15, 18, 20, 22, 24, 41, 43, 51, 55, 70, 74

Yergin, Daniel, xx, 34, 56, 60, 70, 79

Yugoslavia, 1, 76

Yuschenko, Viktor, 60, 62

Z

Zarathustra (Zoroaster), 40, 47

Zarubezneft, 63

Zavtra (Tomorrow), 41

Zenit St. Petersburg, 26

Zyuganov, Gennadi, 41, 42, 70, 77

About the Author

Dr. Peter J. Piveronus, Jr. is currently Adjunct Professor of History and Humanities (Ret.) at Lansing Community College, Lansing, Michigan. Born in Boston, Massachusetts, he has degrees from Boston University and Michigan State University where he received his Ph.D. He is the author of an earlier work, *The Reinvention of Capitalism: Russia's Alternative to Corporate Concentration and to the Command Economy*. He lives in Okemos, Michigan with his wife, Elizabeth.

AUG 09 2009